good goats

HEALING OUR IMAGE OF GOD

Dennis Linn
Sheila Fabricant Linn
Matthew Linn

Illustrations by
Francisco Miranda

Paulist Press
Mahwah/New York

Acknowledgements

We wish to gratefully acknowledge the following persons, who gave us their time and loving car[e] in reading this manuscript and making helpful suggestions: Rev. Stephen Deak; Rev. Robert Faricy, S.J.; D[r.] Morton Kelsey; Francisco Miranda; Rev. Kelly Nemeck, O.M.I.; Rev. Richard Rohr, O.F.M.; Barbara Shlemc[] Ryan, R.N.; Joe and Judy Ryan; Rev. John Sachs, S.J.; Rev. Robert Sears, S.J.; Rev. Paul Smith; and Dr. Dia[ne] Villegas.

Some of this material originally appeared in the following books by the authors: *Healing th[e] Greatest Hurt; Healing the Eight Stages of Life;* and *Belonging: Bonds of Healing & Recovery.* It is reprinted here with permission of the publisher, Paulist Press.

Scripture quotations are from the *New Revised Standard Version,* unless indicated otherwise.

The publisher gratefully acknowledges use of excerpts from the following sources: *God of Surprises* by Gerard W. Hughes, S.J. Copyright © 1985 by Gerard W. Hughes, S.J. Reprinted by permission of Darton Longman & Todd Ltd. *Redemptive Intimacy: A New Perspective for the Journey to Adult Faith,* copyright © 1981, Twenty-Third Publications, Mystic, CT, paper, 176 pp., $5.95. Used by permission. "An Ancient Gift, a Thing of Joy," by James Tunstead Burtchaell, C.S.C., *Notre Dame* Magazine (Winter 1985-86); also found in *Philemon's Problem: The Daily Dilemma of the Christian,* copyright © 1973. Reprinted from *Notre Dame* Magazine and used with permission of the author. *Women and the Word* by Sandra M. Schneiders. Copyright © 1986 by Saint Mary's College, Notre Dame, Ind. Reprinted by permission of Paulist Press.

Book Design by Saija Autrand, Faces Type & Design.

IMPRIMI POTEST:
Bert Thelen, S.J.
Provincial, Wisconsin Province of the Society of Jesus
March 8, 1993

Library of Congress Cataloging-in-Publication Data

Linn, Dennis.
    Good goats : healing our image of God / Dennis Linn, Sheila Fabricant Linn, Matthew Linn.
      p. cm.
    Includes bibliographical references.
    ISBN 0-8091-3463-2 (pbk.)
    1. God—Love. 2. Judgment Day—Biblical teaching. 3. Image of God. 4. Femininity of God. 5. Future punishment—Christianity—Controversial literature. 6. Hell—Christianity—Controversial literature. 7. Catholic Church—Doctrines. I. Linn, Sheila Fabricant. II. Linn, Matthew. III. Title.
BT140.L53 1994
231—dc20
        93-41067
        CIP

Published by Paulist Press
997 Macarthur Boulevard
Mahwah, N.J. 07430

Printed and bound in the United States of America

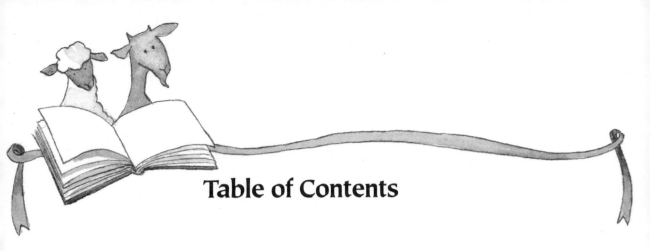

Table of Contents

Note to the Reader v

Dedication vi

Part I: Healing Our Image of God 1

Good Old Uncle George 3

Why Wasn't I Healed? 4

We Become Like the God We Adore 7

How My Image of God Changed 8

God Loves Us at Least As Much As the Person
Who Loves Us the Most 11

What About Vengeful Punishment
in Scripture? 12

Jesus' Response to Vengeful Punishment 14

Reading Vengeful Punishment Passages Literally
Can Drive Us Crazy 17

God's Twenty-Thousand-Year Pout.....................18

Is God a Prosecuting Attorney or a
Defense Attorney?.....................................21

How Being Loved and Forgiven,
as an Unrepentant Sinner, Healed Me.................25

Does God Send Anyone to Hell? 28

What About the Hell of Suffering?....................30

Jesus Comes To Be with Us in Hell....................32

What About Free Will?................................34

The Seed of God......................................36

"God Is a Father; More Than That,
God Is a Mother" 39

Why Is It So Important To Change Our
Image of God?..42

Does Fear of Hell Cause Addiction
and Negative Behaviors? 44

Punishment Never Heals, Only Love Can Heal 46

We Are All Good Goats...............................49

A Simple Way To Change Our Image of God.........50

Part II: Questions & Answers

Part II: Questions & Answers.........................53

Sources...91

Resources for Further Growth........................98

Note to the Reader

This book is based upon a presentation we have given at retreats for several years. Because the material seems different from what many people were taught, we usually receive questions at the end of our presentation. Thus, this book is divided into two parts. The first part, "Healing Our Image of God," contains the simple stories included in our retreat presentation. The second part, "Questions & Answers," contains the way we respond to the questions we most commonly receive, as well as more technical and scholarly information. This section gives the theological foundation for the first part. Bibliographical references are given under Sources.

While we respect your questions, we also want to assure you that what we have written here is well within the parameters of orthodoxy of many Christian traditions, including our own Roman Catholic tradition. Otherwise, this book could not have been published, since our work must be checked for orthodoxy before we can receive an *Imprimi Potest* from the Society of Jesus. Our perspective on the mysteries of heaven and hell is not the only valid perspective, but it is one entirely orthodox perspective.

Dennis Linn
Sheila Fabricant Linn
Matthew Linn, S.J.

Dedication

When the Son of Man comes in his glory... all the nations will be gathered before him and he will separate people one from another as a shepherd separates the sheep from the goats, and he will put the sheep at his right hand and the goats at the left. Then the King will say to those at his right hand, "Come, you that are blessed by my Father, inherit the kingdom prepared for you from the foundation of the world...." Then he will say to those at his left hand, "You that are accursed, depart from me into the eternal fire prepared for the devil and his angels...." And these will go away into eternal punishment, but the righteous into eternal life. (Mt. 25:31-34, 41, 46)

This book is dedicated to anyone who has ever felt like a goat and feared eternal punishment.

Part I

Healing Our Image of God

Good Old Uncle George

I (Dennis) grew up with an image of God that resembled Good Old Uncle George, as described by Gerard Hughes.

God was a family relative, much admired by Mum and Dad, who described him as very loving, a great friend of the family, very powerful and interested in all of us. Eventually we are taken to visit "Good Old Uncle George." He lives in a formidable mansion, is bearded, gruff and threatening. We cannot share our parents' professed admiration for this jewel in the family. At the end of the visit, Uncle George addressed us. "Now listen, dear," he begins, looking very severe, "I want to see you here once a week, and if you fail to come, let me just show you what will happen to you." He then leads us down to the mansion's basement. It is dark, becomes hotter and hotter as we descend, and we begin to hear unearthly screams. In the basement there are steel doors. Uncle George opens one. "Now look in there, dear," he says. We see a nightmare vision, an array of blazing furnaces with little demons in attendance, who hurl into the blaze those men, women and children who failed to visit Uncle George or to act in a way he approved. "And if you don't visit me, dear, that is where you will most certainly go," says Uncle George. He then takes us upstairs again to meet Mum and Dad. As we go home, tightly clutching Dad with one hand and Mum with the other, Mum leans over us and says, "And now don't you love Uncle George with all your heart and soul, mind and strength?" And we, loathing the monster, say, "Yes I do," because to say anything else would be to join the queue at the furnace. At a tender age religious schizophrenia has set in and we keep telling Uncle George how much we love him and how good he is and that we want to do only what pleases him. We observe what we are told are his wishes and dare not admit, even to ourselves, that we loathe him.

Why Wasn't I Healed?

For many years the three of us have prayed for healing of life's crippling hurts. We have experienced profound healing in our own lives and in the lives of others. But I (Dennis) finally came up against a problem in my life where healing prayer didn't work. Why not?

I am half German. Although I don't want to stereotype all Germans, like many of my ancestors I was born a self-righteous German. Like self-righteous "Good Old Uncle George," who threw into the blazing fire anyone who did not act in a way he approved, I, too, saw all the mistakes and errors in everyone but myself.

For years I tried every kind of healing prayer in order to be rid of my self-righteousness. Although these prayers healed me of many things, my self-righteousness did not change. I often wondered why, when I prayed so hard, God did not heal me.

Then one day, I noticed that my self-righteousness had nearly disappeared. Why, I asked, after so many years of struggle, was there suddenly and almost automatically such a wonderful change in my life?

We Become Like the God We Adore

I changed when my image of God changed. Most of us recognize that we become like our parents whom from early on we adore, even with all their faults. We may not realize that we also become like the God we adore.

Unfortunately, the God I grew up adoring was German. My God was a self-righteous German who sat on his (at the time my God was all male) judgment throne. Being a self-righteous German, my God could see all the mistakes and errors in everyone else. If my self-righteous God did not like what he saw in others, he could even separate himself from them by sending them into hell. And if my God could be a self-righteous German, then no matter how many healing prayers I prayed, I would probably never change. I became like the God I adored.

In every aspect of our lives, we become like the God we adore. For example, in a time when we have the capacity to annihilate one another with nuclear weapons, many churches have issued pastoral letters on peace. Our church's pastoral letter says that we can never use nuclear weapons against our enemies. However, if my God can send God's enemies to a hell inferno, then I can send a nuclear inferno on my enemies. But if my God doesn't treat people that way, I can't either. We find that a key to personal and social healing is healing our image of God.

How My Image of God Changed

One day Hilda came to me crying because her son had tried to commit suicide for the fourth time. She told me that he was involved in prostitution, drug dealing and murder. She ended her list of her son's "big sins" with, "What bothers me most is that my son says he wants nothing to do with God. What will happen to my son if he commits suicide without repenting and wanting nothing to do with God?"

Since at the time my image of God was like Good Old Uncle George, I thought, "God will probably send your son to hell." But I didn't want to tell Hilda that. I was glad that my many years of theological training had taught me what to do when I don't know how to answer a difficult theological question: ask the other person, "What do you think?"

"Well," Hilda responded, "I think that when you die, you appear before the judgment seat of God. If you have lived a good life, God will send you to heaven. If you have lived a bad life, God will send you to hell." Sadly, she concluded, "Since my son has lived such a bad life, if he were to die without repenting, God would certainly send him to hell."

Although I tended to agree with her, I didn't want to say, "Right on, Hilda! Your son would probably be sent to hell." I was again grateful for my theological training which taught me a second strategy: when you don't know how to solve a theological problem, then let God solve it. So I said to Hilda, "Close your eyes. Imagine that you are sitting next to the judgment seat of God. Imagine also that your son has died with all these serious sins and without repenting. He has just arrived at the judgment seat of God. Squeeze my hand when you can imagine that."

A few minutes later Hilda squeezed my hand. She described to me the entire judgment scene. Then I asked her, "Hilda, how does your son feel?" Hilda answered, "My son feels so lonely and empty." I asked Hilda what she would like to do. She said, "I want to throw my arms around my son." She lifted her arms and began to cry as she imagined herself holding her son tightly.

Finally, when she had stopped crying, I asked her to look into God's eyes and watch what God wanted to do. God stepped down from the throne, and just as Hilda did, embraced Hilda's son. And the three of them, Hilda, her son and God, cried together and held one another.

God Loves Us at Least As Much As the Person Who Loves Us the Most

I was stunned. What Hilda taught me in those few minutes is the bottom line of healthy Christian spirituality: God loves us at least as much as the person who loves us the most. God loves us at least as much as Hilda loves her son or at least as much as Sheila and Matt love me.

When Sheila and Matt most love me, they are not going to say, "Dennis, we love you unconditionally, much more than you can ever imagine. But you really blew it. So, to hell with you, but remember how much we love you." And even though Sheila has a mighty big purse, she does not lug around an account book to mark down my sins and what punishment I merit. And if Sheila and Matt don't do these things, could it be that God doesn't either?

What About Vengeful Punishment in Scripture?

At first I found it hard to believe in Hilda's loving God. I had grown up reading Matthew 25, about what God would do to goats, and other seemingly vengeful punishment passages in scripture. For example, Matthew 5:29 says that if your right eye is a temptation, it would be better to pluck it out than to have God throw you into the fires of hell. Such passages made God seem to be a child abuser, much like Good Old Uncle George.

Assuming that what I had learned from Hilda might be true, I began asking myself, how do those who love us the most use vengeful punishment language? Then I began to notice that those who love the most—grandparents, parents, lovers—often use the same words of vengeful punishment as Good Old Uncle George and other child abusers, but their meaning is very different.

For example, our cousins Ann and George have raised four of the healthiest teenagers we know. We often ask Ann and George, "How did you do it?" One time we asked them, "Can you remember a time in the past year when you punished your kids?" They both looked blank. In desperation we asked, "When in the past five or ten years have you punished your kids?" They looked at each other and came up with the same thing. Ann said, "I remember a family trip. It got so loud in the back seat of the car that George said, 'If you kids don't be quiet, I'm going to tie you to the roof of the car!' And do you remember, George, how quiet it got?"

About that time their son, Joe, came home. We asked him when his parents had last punished him and at first got the same blank look. Finally, we asked him, "Joe, can you remember any time at all in the past five or ten years

when your parents punished you?" Joe's face lit up. "You remember when we were in the car on a trip and we were making so much noise? Dad, you told us that if we weren't quiet, you'd tie us to the roof of the car!" Then Joe added, "And, boy, were we quiet. But we knew you weren't going to tie us to the roof of the car." And they all laughed.

To tie your children to the roof of a car is vengeful punishment. Yet we use vengeful punishment language all the time in our homes and families. Such statements are exaggerations (hyperbole) that can safely be used only in a context where everyone understands that they are not to be taken literally. (The authors of scripture and Jesus himself often used hyperbole, as in Matthew 5:29. The people of their time understood that they were not to be taken literally.) Like Joe, we know that if at the time people use such language they are really loving us, then they will never carry out the punishment. Everyone involved knows that the language is used only in order to emphasize the importance of doing something so that we can enjoy being together. Thus George's angry words in the car probably meant, "It's important that you be quiet so that we can enjoy the trip together." And in Mt. 5:29, instead of commanding us to pluck out our right eye, God may well be saying something like, "It's important that you not misuse your sight through lust (that you not damage your right eye—the window to your heart) so that we can enjoy the inner beauty of creation together."

But what if Ann and George were child abusers who did tie their kids to the roof of the car? If we overheard them threatening to do that to their children, we would call the police. We would have the police come and put Ann and George (or Good Old Uncle George, for that matter) in a mental institution before they could do more harm to their children. But the good news is that God is at least as loving as Ann and George. Like them, God is not a child abuser but a child lover.

Jesus' Response to Vengeful Punishment

Changing our image of God from child abuser to child lover was the core of Jesus' mission. Jesus was always trying to change people's vengeful image of God. Often Jesus tried to heal on the sabbath, or touch a leper, or forgive someone. But the priests, scribes, and Pharisees would forbid Jesus to do these things because they interpreted literally the vengeful punishment passages of their Bibles which spelled out the consequences of such "illegal" actions.

For example, in the story of the adulterous woman (Jn. 8:5), the scribes and Pharisees want to stone her to death. They justify themselves by telling Jesus, "Moses has ordered us in the law to condemn women like this to death by stoning" (Jn. 8:5). They are referring to the law of Moses (Lv. 20:10, Dt. 22:20), which says that God orders the vengeful punishment of stoning to death an adulterous woman. If Jesus, like the scribes and Pharisees, read scripture's vengeful punishment passages literally, he too would have had to join the scribes and Pharisees in stoning the adulterous woman. When he invites the scribes and Pharisees to put down their stones, he is inviting them to stop reading the vengeful punishment passages of the Bible literally.

Reading Vengeful Punishment Passages Literally Can Drive Us Crazy

The time when I understood most clearly the dangers of reading the vengeful punishment passages in the Bible literally was when I was called to a mental hospital to see my friend, Bill Wilson. Guards ushered me into his room. Bill's hands were chained to his bed and he had a bandage over the right side of his face. That morning he had tried to gouge out his right eye. When I asked him why, he quoted to me Matthew 5:29, "If your right eye causes you to sin, tear it out and throw it away; it is better for you to lose one of your members than for your whole body to be thrown into hell."

Everyone knew Bill was crazy for taking the first part of that passage, "If your right eye causes you to sin, tear it out and throw it away," so literally. But I realized that Bill was no more crazy for taking the first part of that passage literally than I was for taking the second part literally and believing that God would vengefully throw me into hell.

Bill was no more crazy than I was as an adolescent when I walked into a gas station and saw a calendar with a picture of a nude woman on it. I thought, "Now I have committed a mortal sin, and if after leaving here I am involved in a car accident and die, I will go directly to hell." And Bill was no more crazy than the many parents I have overheard saying to their children, "You better behave or God is going to punish you."

God's Twenty-Thousand-Year Pout

My tendency to read the vengeful punishment language in scripture literally came in part from a common understanding of the teaching of St. Anselm (1033–1109). In *Redemptive Intimacy*, Dick Westley quotes theologian Walter Imbiorski who describes how Anselm's thinking has often been caricatured by popular Christian teaching:

> You see, part of the difficulty is that most of us are caught up emotionally in what I would call Anselmian Salvation Theology, which goes something like this. God created the world. Adam and Eve sinned. God got pretty damn sore, goes into a 10,000 year pout, slams the gates of heaven and throws the scoundrels out. So he's up there pouting and about 5,000 years go by and the Son comes up and gives him the elbow and says: "Hey Dad, now is the time to forgive those people down there." God says, "No. I don't like them, they offended my divine majesty, they stay out. Let's make another galaxy instead!" Five thousand more years go by and the Son comes up and says: "Aw come on, Dad, let's forgive them! Look, I tell you what I'm going to do. If you will love them again, I'll go down there and become one of them, then you'll have to love them because I'll be one of them." God looks at the Son and says: "Don't bank on it. That doesn't turn me on too much at all." So the Son replies, "All right, God-Father, I'll tell you what I'm going to do. I'll raise the ante. I'll make you an offer you can't refuse! I'll not only go down there and become one of them, I'll suffer for them, real blood—you know how that turns you on, Dad! How about it?" And God says: "Now you're talking. But it's

got to be real torture and real blood—no God-tricks you understand. You've got to really suffer. And if you'll do that then I'll forgive them. But if they stray off the straight and narrow just that much—ZAP—I'm going to send them to hell so fast their heads will swim." And that is what we have been calling the "good news" of the Gospel.

Is God a Prosecuting Attorney or a Defense Attorney?

The theology of Anselm leaves out some very important "good news" because it ignores other traditional and more compassionate understandings of the New Testament accounts. For example, *parakletos,* or the "Spirit of Jesus that judges us" could best be translated as "our defense attorney who justifies us" (Jn. 14:15, Jn. 15:26). Spanish conveys this well, since in many biblical translations and church prayers it describes the Spirit of Jesus which judges as *nuestro abogado,* meaning "our defense attorney."

The New Testament has many stories of Jesus as defense attorney. Two such stories are those of St. Paul (Acts 9:1-22) and of the adulterous woman (Jn. 8:2-12). In refusing to let anyone else stone or condemn her, Jesus is the adulterous woman's defense attorney. Jesus does judge her, but as a defense attorney, not as a prosecuting attorney. Jesus recognizes and points out the woman's destructive *behavior* (adultery), but he stands unreservedly on her side as a *person.* The people he seems most upset with are the stone-throwers, who are behaving like prosecuting attorneys (Jn. 8:7).

Jesus is also Paul's defense attorney. One could imagine few harder-hearted people than Paul. As a Jewish Pharisee who could see the mistakes and errors in everyone else but himself, Paul suffered an addiction akin to my "German self-righteousness." In addition, Paul behaved like a "rage-aholic" and a "control-aholic." Paul wanted nothing to do with Jesus. He even actively persecuted Jesus (Acts 9:4) and showed no signs of repentance.

What did Jesus do? Jesus loved and healed Paul. Paul's punishing, pharisaical image of God (much like Good Old Uncle George) changed to that of a loving God. In the moment that Paul's image of God changed, Paul changed. Paul began to recover from his addiction to vindictive self-righteousness, violence and murder because he discovered that God wasn't addicted to these things either. And what had Paul done to bring about this healing? Nothing. God had demanded from Paul no prerequisites. No prior repentance, nothing.

The good news of Paul's story and other New Testament stories is not: God loves the repentant sinner. Rather the radical good news is: God loves and heals the unrepentant sinner.

This does not mean repentance is unimportant or meaningless. But it is not the case that we first repent and then God loves us. Rather, it is just the opposite. Paul could repent only because God loved and healed him while he was still unrepentant. The only reason we have the capacity to move from unrepentance to repentance is that God has first loved and healed us (1 Jn. 4:19) while we were unrepentant. Thus repentance is important not in order to earn God's love and forgiveness but rather, as in the case of Paul, to enjoy and fully incorporate into our life the healing that God has initiated.

Jesus does indeed judge Paul and tell Paul all that he's done wrong including how he persecuted Christians (Acts 9:4). But rather than condemn Paul, Jesus understands the "justness" or reasonableness of Paul's life. Jesus as defense attorney can see through to Paul's inner goodness. Healing comes whenever Jesus as defense attorney judges us in such a way that we know we are unconditionally loved.

The summation of Jesus' entire life as defense attorney rather than prosecuting attorney is his final words on the cross. The cross demonstrates two profound realities: the depth of destruction caused by unloving behavior, and the even greater depth of love in God's response. Jesus compassionately bestows his Father's forgiveness on his unrepentant murderers with the words of a defense attorney: "Father, forgive them; for they do not know what they are doing" (Lk. 23:34).

How Being Loved and Forgiven, as an Unrepentant Sinner, Healed Me

Being loved as an unrepentant sinner, as Paul was, has often been a healing and life-changing experience for me. For example, years ago my German self-righteousness got set off by the U.S. border patrol. One day, while we were in California a mile from the Mexican border, I was writing outside with Sheila. We saw the border guards catch five Mexicans on the beach. We wanted to reach out to the Mexicans in some way, so we went inside the house, gathered up enough granola bars for them, and went out to the beach. When we arrived, the five Mexicans had their hands up in the air and were being searched. We had just been in Mexico, where we felt overwhelmed by meeting so many jobless people unable to provide adequate food for their hungry families. Thus we understood why these Mexicans were fleeing. Yet the border guards treated their prisoners impersonally, never asking who they were or why they had come. I was so upset at the guards that even though they addressed me several times in a friendly manner, I responded coldly. All I could do was offer the Mexicans our granola bars and apologize for the impersonal way the border guards were treating them.

Arriving back home, I could smell the quiche Matt was making us for lunch. I told Matt what had happened and asked him why he hadn't come. Matt said, "Dennis, when you came in to get those granola bars, you were so hostile toward the border guards, I wouldn't have gone anywhere with you." Matt had spoken the truth. I was right in being angry at how impersonally the guards were treating the prisoners. But I was wrong in hostilely acting out that anger and treating the border guards in the same impersonal way. In responding coldly, even when the guards spoke to me in a friendly way, I had cut off the possibility of influencing their behavior toward the Mexicans. So, once again we loaded up with granola bars. This time, we went to the border guards and apologized for treating them so impersonally. As we ate granola bars together, the border guards eventually shared how they didn't like capturing jobless Mexicans. However, they needed their guard jobs to support their own families. As I asked forgiveness for treating them impersonally, they were able to open themselves to our suggestions for treating Mexicans more personally.

I could hear the truth of Matt's judgment about treating the border guards impersonally because I could smell the quiche that Matt had baked for us and experience his love that would never reject me. I could also hear the truth of Matt's judgment because he had been with us in Mexico. Thus, like a defense attorney, Matt understood the "justness" or "reasonableness" of my anger. Being filled with Matt's love, even as he judged my behavior, healed me and gave me power to repent. It gave me the desire to bring that same love to the border guards as I asked them to forgive me. Thus Matt's love, as in the case of Jesus loving Paul, was not dependent upon my having repented. Rather, his love healed me so that I could repent and even become aware of destructive behavior that I was previously unable to see, like treating the border guards impersonally.

Does God Send Anyone to Hell?

Our Roman Catholic tradition and many other Christian traditions share two beliefs about afterlife. The first belief is that heaven exists and people are there. (By "heaven" we don't mean a specific geographical place "up there," but rather a state of loving union with God.) We all have loved ones—grandparents, parents, friends—who we are confident are in heaven. Secondly, hell exists as a possibility, but we don't know if anyone is there. (By "hell," we mean a state of supreme alienation.) If anyone is in hell, it is not because God sent that person there, but because he or she chose it. C.S. Lewis used the image of hell as a room with the door closed from the inside, our side. But, as theologian Richard McBrien writes, "neither Jesus, nor the Church after him, ever stated that persons go there or are actually there now." We know only that we are not to judge, and we are to pray that all of us open our hearts to God.

What hope do we have that all people will open their hearts to God? What happens when we die? The Christian God is an expert at opening hearts. For example, we read how God, in Jesus, did thou-

sands of miracles in just three years' time. Many of them were with hard-hearted people, like Paul, who wanted nothing to do with Jesus. When we die, we will have not just three years but a whole eternity of God's loving and healing initiatives. Even if we were to die as hard-hearted as Paul, God would spend eternity trying to love and heal us. We know this because God's essence is love (1 Jn. 4:16) and love heals. God has no other choice but to spend eternity loving and healing us (1 Cor. 13). Hope in God's healing initiatives to save everyone is central to the Gospel message:

> And I—when I am lifted up from the earth— will draw all people to myself (Jn. 12:32).

> When all things are subjected to him, then the Son himself will also be subjected to the one who put all things in subjection under him, so that God may be all in all (1 Cor. 15:28).

Perhaps because of Paul's personal experience of being loved and healed as an unrepentant sinner, he (like other authors of scripture) includes the hope that God's healing initiatives will ultimately bring all of us home (in addition to 1 Cor. 15:28, see Rom. 5:12–21, 11:30–32; 1 Cor. 15:22; Eph. 1:10; 1 Tim. 2:3–6, 4:10; Phil. 2:10–11; Col. 1:19–20; 1 Thess. 5:9; Titus 2:11; Heb. 2:9; Jn. 1:9, 1:29, 3:17, 12:47b; 1 Jn. 2:2; Rev. 5:13).

Some people say, "But we don't have a whole eternity. We make a free definitive decision at death, when we choose either heaven or hell forever." Since none of us has died, none of us can know this with certainty. But let's just imagine that what they say is true. This would mean that at the moment of death we would have to experience a whole eternity of God's healing initiatives, because we cannot freely and definitively turn down what we have not experienced. Ultimately, our hope is not in the life we have lived, but rather in the healing initiatives of God who will spend eternity loving and healing us.

What About the Hell of Suffering?

If God is so willing to spend eternity loving and healing us, where is God when we suffer now? If God abandons us to the hell of suffering in this world, how can we believe God won't abandon us to hell in the next? Where is God in natural disasters, wars, tragic accidents, concentration camps? Job, after losing his health, home and family, concluded that suffering was a mystery in which we cannot know the role of God (Job 42:1-6). Elie Wiesel, watching the Nazis hang an innocent child in the hell of the holocaust, came to a different conclusion:

> Total silence throughout the camp. On the horizon,
> the sun was setting. "Bare your heads!", yelled the

head of the camp. His voice was raucous. We were weeping. "Cover your heads!"

Then the march past began. The two adults were no longer alive. Their tongues hung swollen, blue-tinged. But the third rope was still moving; being so light, the child was still alive....

For more than half an hour he stayed there, struggling between life and death, dying in slow agony under our eyes. And we had to look him full in the face. He was still alive when I passed in front of him. His tongue was still red, his eyes were not yet glazed. Behind me I heard [a] man asking, "Where is God now?"

And I heard a voice within me answer him: "Where is He? Here He is—He is hanging here on this gallows."

Jesus Comes To Be with Us in Hell

What if it appears that some people, such as Hitler or the Nazis who hung the innocent child before Elie Wiesel's eyes, have closed the door of their heart from the inside, and chosen hell? Is there anything God can do? By descending into hell, God can come to heal us even there. The common understanding of Jesus' descent into hell (1 Pt. 3:19) is that

Jesus goes to preach the good news only to the just souls awaiting redemption. However, according to the *New Jerusalem Bible,* this understanding overlooks that Jesus goes also to the chained demons mentioned in the Book of Enoch and those in Noah's time who were punished by the flood because they "refused to believe."

Theologian Hans Urs von Balthasar asserts that Jesus' descent into hell, commemorated each Holy Saturday, signifies Jesus' utter solidarity with sinners. As the expression of God's infinitely merciful love for sinners, Jesus identifies completely with them, to the point of dying on the cross as one of them. Seemingly abandoned by God, Jesus cries out, "My God, my God, why have you forsaken me?" In this moment Jesus experiences the "hell" of God's absence more acutely than would be possible for any other person.

Then, on Holy Saturday, Jesus goes to be with sinners in still another way, in what we call his descent into hell. If we define hell as the adamant choice to close one's heart to God, then it would seem that hell is the one place where God cannot be. By going there anyway, Jesus refuses to accept that choice and expresses God's adamant unwillingness to leave us to our own worst selves. Von Balthasar says,

> And exactly in that way, he disturbs the absolute loneliness striven for by the sinner: the sinner, who wants to be "damned" apart from God, finds God again in his loneliness, but God in the absolute weakness of love who unfathomably in the period of nontime enters into solidarity with those damning themselves. The words of the Psalm, "If I make my bed in the netherworld, thou art there" (Ps. 139:8), thereby take on a totally new meaning.

Loving friends and family will not leave a suicidal person to his or her worst self. They will do everything possible to enter into that person's hell in order to intervene and stop that person from taking his or her own life. In a similar way, Jesus' descent into hell is his refusal to accept our choice of destruction. Holy Saturday proclaims that Jesus' mission is to demonstrate solidarity with us by even, if necessary, descending into our hell and being with us there until his healing presence renews us enough to rise with him on Easter.

What About Free Will?

Does Jesus' descent into hell to be with those who seem to have rejected God violate free will? Or, could it be that by his loving and healing presence to those in hell, Jesus restores free will? Free will has often been defined as the capacity to say "Yes" or "No" to God. However, Karl Rahner and other theologians suggest that free will is the capacity to choose in a God-like way. Thus a truly free person paradoxically, like God, can only choose the good. Saying "No" to God is not a sign of free will but rather of how a person still needs healing in order to become free. Once healed and truly free, that person, like Jesus, can only say "Yes" to God. Thus, summarizing Rahner, John Sachs writes,

> ... human freedom is simply and most radically the capacity for God, not the capacity for *either* God or something else. Human freedom is created for one end alone: God. Only God finally "defines" the human person. Therefore, it would seem that human freedom can attain real finality only when it reaches the definitiveness for which it is specifically created.

The Seed of God

Meister Eckhart put it this way:

The seed of God is in us.
Now
    the seed of a pear tree
      grows into a pear tree;
and a hazel seed
    grows into a hazel tree;

a seed of God
    grows into
      God.

"God Is a Father;
More Than That, God Is a Mother"
(John Paul I)

At times I (Dennis) resisted changing my image of God from that of child abuser to child lover. At first I thought that my resistance was to changing my theology. But I discovered that my real resistance was to changing my personality.

First, to stop reading scripture so literally and to begin to appreciate its images and symbols, I needed to rely less on my ability to think and more on my underdeveloped feeling side. Secondly, to appreciate how God loves the unrepentant sinner, how grace is not earned but given as a free gift, I had to become more at home with *receiving* from others rather than always compulsively *doing* things for them. In summary, I needed to integrate feminine values into my deeply skewed male value system.

I grew up with a male skew. I was good at efficiency, building things in the outer world, competing, and dominating my environment. I believed that external authorities had all the answers. Heaven and hell were places "out there." Like many men, I was oriented toward *outer* space. I was not so good at the feminine values of caring for things as they are, mutuality or experiencing my own feelings and body wisdom. I didn't know that truth is also found within, and that heaven and hell have an inner meaning, as measures of my own connectedness or disconnectedness to God, myself, others and the entire universe. I was out of touch with the feminine dimension of *inner* space.

In order to become a more balanced person, I needed to develop my feminine side, and in order to develop my feminine side I needed to know God the Mother. All language for God is metaphorical; God is not literally a father. But if God is *like* a father, then God is also *like* a mother. Male and female, loving mothers and fathers reflect for us equally the image of God (Gen. 1:27). Why is this so important?

Just as we become like our human parents, we also become like the God we adore. If we were raised only by a human father and never knew a mother, it is likely that our feminine side will be undeveloped. In the same way, if we know only God the Father and not also God the Mother, it is likely that our feminine side will be undeveloped and that our emotional and spiritual life will have a masculine skew, as mine did.

But I am changing as people like Sheila and Hilda introduce me to the feminine side of God. In embracing her unrepentant son, Hilda personified for me what John Paul II referred to as *rahamim,* or the tender compassion coming from the motherly side of God. The root of *rahamim* is the Hebrew noun *rehem,* meaning "womb" or "uterus." This motherly womb-love of God is expressed in Isaiah 49:15: "Can a mother forget her infant, or be without tenderness for the child of her womb? Even should she forget you, I will never forget you." Such womb-love is gut energy. Not filtered through the head, it has nothing to do with decision or merit. As in Hilda's case, it comes from interior necessity; a real mother "can't help but love the brat." In other words, just as God is more father than any father, God is also more mother than any mother.

When Hilda discovered that the deepest movement of her heart, her "womb-love" for her child, was an expression of God's love, and that her desire to embrace her son was God's desire, she was introducing me to the feminine side of God and teaching me to perceive God in a feminine way. My masculine emphasis on outer space had affected my way of perceiving God. I had known mainly the transcendent God, who was found "out there." My God was the infinitely mighty one who is beyond anything or anyone else, the "King" and "Lord" of the Christian hymns I grew up singing. This God was always ahead of me, calling me to change and to grow. In contrast, Hilda's connection with her inner space revealed to me a God who is immanent and lives within the deepest movements of my heart. This God loves me exactly as I am, without needing to fix or change me. When the masculine within me was not balanced by the feminine, it became a caricature of itself rather than the beauty and strength of true masculinity.

When I don't have both sides of God, I easily get fixated in a male way of being. A symptom of such fixation would be the thought that "God will certainly send Hilda's son to hell." Such thinking ascribes to God my male overemphasis on dominance, control and competition, in which there are clear winners and losers.

As long as we have an all-male God, what happened to me will also happen to our culture and our church. Their values too will be those of domination and competition, in which we devalue women, do not develop our feminine side, and do not trust or cherish the inner life of ourselves or others. And so long as we believe our culture when it tells us that it is good to dominate and be in control, we will reinforce our exclusively male image of God.

Why Is It So Important
To Change Our Image of God?

Why is it so important to heal our image of God? It is not so we'll know what afterlife is like. Rather, it is because we become like the God we adore. Studies show this is true in many aspects of our lives. In marriage, for example, the more a couple experiences God as a lover, the more likely they are to enjoy a wholesome, loving marriage. Andrew Greeley found that this wholesomeness extends to all aspects of marriage, including sexual fulfillment. So, too, in David Nygren and Miriam Ukeritis' study of who are the most caring and least caring among those who choose celibate religious life, the most caring were four times more likely to image God as a caring healer than their less caring peers. Andrew Greeley also found that the more we experience God as a lover, the more sensitive we are to social justice.

Not just world peace, as we mentioned earlier, but every social justice issue is affected by our image of God. For example, the Roman Catholic bishops recently issued a pastoral letter on the economy which says that wealth or goods cannot be divided on the basis of what we merit through our work. Rather, they must be divided on the basis of what we need. But what if we have a vengeful, punishing God who calculates on the basis of our work exactly what we merit as eternal reward or punishment? In this case, we will probably choose an economic system that is also based on merit. We can easily say to those who have less, "To hell with you, we earned it." But when God becomes a lover generously giving free gifts to those working only an hour (Mt. 20:1-16), and even to unrepentant sinners solely because they need it, then we are likely to choose an economic system based less on merit and more on need.

Similarly, if we believe God gives up on people forever and does away with them by sentencing them to death in hell, then we can give up on some people forever and do away with such people by sentencing them to death through capital punishment. But when God doesn't give up, then we are more likely to question capital punishment or any other option in which we might be tempted to give up forever on people who are threatening to us.

Whatever our addiction as a society, whether it be to violence and retribution as opposed to peace and compassion, or to hoarding money as opposed to sharing, we usually mimic the addictions we attribute to the God we adore.

Does Fear of Hell Cause Addiction and Negative Behaviors?

Whether our addiction be work, money, smoking, drinking, or Dennis' German self-righteousness, we get stuck in addictions for the same reason that alcoholic Bill Wilson, the co-founder of Alcoholics Anonymous, took his first drink: to deaden the pain of not belonging. Before his first drink, the socially awkward Bill W. knew well the pain of not belonging. After his first drink everything changed. Bill became the life of the party and he said, "For the first time I felt that I belonged." What followed was seventeen years of compulsive drinking, trying to recapture that first drink's feeling of belonging. Finally, when he was thirty-nine and on the verge of being institutionalized for chronic alcoholism, Bill cried out to God for help. Suddenly his room filled with light and Bill felt a presence which "seemed like a veritable sea of living spirit." Bill described this experience in almost the same words he used after his first drink, "For the first time I felt that I really belonged." Bill never took another drink. He began drinking because it was the best way he knew at the time to belong, and he stopped drinking when he found a better way to belong, through his conversion experience of a loving God. We believe that the feeling of not belonging underlies every addiction. Every addiction (or compulsive negative behavior) began as the best way we knew at the time to belong to ourselves, others, God and the universe. The way out of an addiction is to find a better way to belong.

If we have a God who can send us to hell, who can vengefully decide who doesn't belong, then we are more likely to become addicted people. Treatment centers recognize this addictive cycle. Dr. Robert Stuckey, whose recovery units have treated over 20,000 addicts, found that the recovery rate is much lower for addicts with a fearful and punishing image of God. He concludes that addicts in treatment "with a very harsh view of God have a harder time than people with no religious training at all." Bill W. spoke of how in recovery, we generally change our image of God many times. But he concluded that once we discover a God of "belonging," "all will be well with us here and hereafter."

Punishment Never Heals,
Only Love Can Heal

When we speak of how our recovery depends so much on knowing God as merciful and loving, the most frequent question we are asked is this: "If God is so merciful and loving, then why be good?" I (Dennis) understand this question since I did many good things because I feared a vengeful, punishing God. For example, I read Matthew 25 about the sheep and the goats. I interpreted this passage literally and thought that since the sheep go to heaven and the goats go to hell, I wanted to make sure I was a sheep. So, out of fear and as a good sheep, I did many good things such as visiting the sick and feeding the hungry. Yet, when my image of God changed, I did even more good things and did them with more love. We do the most loving actions for those we love the most, not for those we fear the most. I do more for Sheila and Matt than for anyone else.

We can scare people into changing their behavior through fear of hell or fear of losing love. In fact, fear may have to be used occasionally on an emergency basis. For example, a family might tell their alcoholic father that unless he changes they are going to leave in order to protect themselves from his behavior. By appealing to his fear of not belonging, this family might get the alcoholic to stop drinking. But unless the alcoholic's fear is eventually replaced with a deep sense of love and belonging, he will replace drinking with other addictions. Through fear we can temporarily change a person's behavior, but only love and belonging can ultimately change the person.

I (Sheila) grew up in the Jewish tradition, where we were not taught "the fear of hell." It would never have occurred to the Jews in my community to scare people into being good. We were taught that people, although wounded and imperfect, were naturally good. If they did something that wasn't so good, it was only because they were hurt and scared. We knew that what these scared people needed wasn't more fear, but rather more love and care from all of us. Unloving behavior is not ok. But what heals it permanently is love, not fear. As Bill W. said, "Punishment never heals. Only love can heal."

We Are All Good Goats

A few years ago, we presented some of the ideas in this book to a group of elderly retired Roman Catholic nuns. One sister raised her hand and said, "But what about the story of the sheep and the goats? It says right there that the sheep go to heaven and the goats go to hell."

Dennis responded by asking the whole group, "How many of you, even once in your life, have done what Jesus asks at the beginning of that passage and fed a hungry person, clothed a naked person or visited a person in prison?" All the sisters raised their hands. Dennis said, "That's wonderful! You're all sheep." Then Dennis asked, "How many of you, even once in your life, have walked by a hungry person, failed to clothe a naked person, or not visited someone in prison?" Slowly, all the sisters raised their hands. Dennis said, "That's too bad. You're all goats."

The sisters looked worried and perplexed. Then suddenly one very old sister's hand shot up. She blurted out, "I get it! We're all good goats!"

That sister did get it. She understood that language about heaven and hell is symbolic language. Heaven and hell are not specific geographical places. They are symbols of inner realities, of states of being. All of us who have felt alienated, unloved, overwhelmed by shame or helplessly caught in an addiction know what it's like to be in hell. And all of us who have been welcomed home, who have seen our goodness reflected in the affirming eyes of another or who have been loved into recovery know what it's like to be in heaven. We all have wheat and weeds within us, sheep and goats. The kingdom of God is within us, and we're all good goats.

A Simple Way To Change
Our Image of God

Perhaps the easiest way to change our image of God is to try something that takes only a minute.

1. Get in touch with the love of God in your heart.

2. Put a smile on your face that matches that love.

3. Smile at a person who loves you and allow that person to smile back at you.

Taking in the smile of someone who loves us is such a simple thing. Yet, it can be one of the most healing things in life. A friend's smile can heal us if we know that God loves us, just for a start, at least as much as the people who love us the most.

Part II

Questions & Answers

As you read this book, you may have questions, as do many of our retreatants when we present this material. In this section, we have collected the questions we most frequently receive. They are organized under headings used in Part I.

This book is about great mysteries which none of us fully understand. Thus, each of these questions has many possible answers. The one we have given is not intended to be *The* Right Answer, but only our best attempt at *an* answer that is consistent with Christian doctrine. We hope that our attempts will encourage you to reflect upon these questions for yourself and perhaps arrive at answers different from our own.

What About Vengeful Punishment in Scripture?

Question: If I can't just read scripture literally, does that mean I have to be a theologian in order to understand the Bible? How will I ever know what a scripture passage really means?

We don't have to be theologians, but we do have to be in touch with our experience of what helps us to love. A test to discover whether we are properly understanding a scripture passage (or a private revelation such as those given at Fatima or Medjugorje) is to judge our interpretation by its fruits. Since the most important fruit is love, we can ask ourselves, "When someone who loves me is loving me the most, would he or she act in this way?" And, since every authentic aspect of Christianity is good news, we can also ask ourselves, "Is it good news?" If the answers to these questions are "Yes," we probably understand the passage. If not, we are probably making a mistake, such as taking something literally which is really intended as an image.

Down through the centuries, failure to ask such questions has often resulted in literally interpreting scripture. This has caused many abuses, such as the consignment of all Jews to hell at the Council of Florence in 1442, the imprisonment of Galileo, and support for slavery. The scriptural foundation for the inquisition was a literal understanding of "A man who does not live in me is like a withered, rejected branch, picked up to be thrown in the fire and burnt" (John 15:6). Another example is Pope Alexander VI, who took literally, as applying to himself, Matthew 28:18: "All authority in heaven and on earth has been given to me." Alexander therefore decided that he had personal jurisdiction over every human being. So, he gave half of the globe to Portugal and the other half to Spain.

Question: If the scripture passages that speak of punishment are not to be taken literally, are you saying that children or others who misbehave should never be punished?

In saying that people who love us will never carry out a punishment, we are speaking of *vengeful* punishment. We are not speaking of "therapeutic punishment," perhaps better called "correction" or "guidance," since for many people "punishment" connotes violence. In correction or guidance, we provide structure for a child who is physically or emotionally overwhelmed (e.g., sending a child who is overtired and fussy to his or her room for a nap), and/or we ask a child to take responsibililty for the consequences of his or her behavior (e.g., asking a child to make amends for damage to another's property caused by the child's carelessness). Such therapeutic punishment is done lovingly and is intended to enable the child to give and receive more love. Vengeful punishment, on the other hand, is not done lovingly and does not enable anyone to give and receive more love.

Question: Good parents don't make empty threats to their children. Doesn't God mean what God says?

As we have said, exaggeration (or hyperbole) was a common way of speaking in Jesus' culture. When he spoke in ways that seemed to threaten vengeful punishment, Jesus' listeners would have understood that his words were not intended as threats or as predictions of what was inevitably going to happen to them. Rather, such words were intended as warnings, meant to wake us up and deter us from destructive behavior.

Question: If God is a child lover who never vengefully punishes us, how did we ever get cruelty and love so mixed up in our image of God?

Our schizophrenic perception of God as demonstrating love through cruelty is related both as cause and result to equally schizophrenic child-rearing practices. Alice Miller writes,

> "He who spares the rod hates his son, but he who loves him is diligent to discipline him," we read in Proverbs. This so-called wisdom is still so widespread today that we can often hear: A slap given in love does a child no harm. . . . If people weren't accustomed to the biblical injunction from childhood, it would strike them as the untruth it is. Cruelty is the opposite of love, and its traumatic effect, far from being reduced, is actually reinforced if it is presented as a sign of love.
>
> . . . No one ever slaps a child out of love but rather because in similar situations, when one was defenseless, one was slapped and then compelled to interpret it as a sign of love. . . .
>
> If a mother can make it clear to a child that at that particular moment when she slapped him, her love for him deserted her and she was dominated by other feelings that had nothing to do with the child, the child can keep a clear head, feel respected, and not be disoriented in his relationship to his mother.

It may be helpful to reflect on your own childhood experience. Such experience profoundly affects our image of God. If our childhood experience included cruelty and abuse, even by well-intentioned parents who believed the doctrine of "spare the rod . . . ," our image of God is likely to include cruelty and abuse. Children of abusive parents frequently defend and return to those parents because they are the only parents they have. So, too, we are likely to defend and return to an abusive image of God. Moreover, the nature of the cycle of abuse is such that, until we move through denial and face the pain of our own abuse, we will pass on this abuse and cruelty to others, often using an abusive image of God to justify it.

Jesus' Response to Vengeful Punishment

Question: What is your basis for saying that changing our vengeful image of God was the core of Jesus' mission?

Scripture scholars agree that in Luke 4:14-19, Jesus in the Nazareth synagogue proclaimed his own mission using the words of Isaiah 61:1-2. But why, after he proclaimed his mission, was the whole audience filled with indignation to the point of wanting to hurl Jesus over the edge of the mountain (Lk. 4:30)? The Jewish listeners wanted the Messiah to be vengeful to the Romans, to the Sidonians, to the Syrians—to all but themselves. But in quoting Isaiah, Jesus skipped the sentence in 61:2 which speaks of God's vengeance on enemies, and instead declared that God's "favor" rested on all—Romans, Sidonians and Syrians alike (Lk. 4:26-27). Jesus angered his Jewish listeners because he was proclaiming the end of vengeful punishment and the reign of a Messiah whose "favor" shines on the just and the unjust. As Robert Jewett explains, by skipping the sentence regarding God's vengeance and thus placing himself in opposition to the vengeance tradition, Jesus violated the literal interpretation of scripture prevalent in his time.

God's Twenty-Thousand-Year Pout

Question: In questioning Anselmian salvation theology, are you saying there was no need for Jesus to die on the cross for us?

No, what we're saying is that Jesus didn't need to embrace the cross to pay back a God whose love was limited. Rather, Jesus died to convince us that God's love has no limits—not even the limits of dying for us (Rom. 5:6–8). As James Burtchaell puts it, "Jesus' mission is not to represent our interests before the Father, but to disclose his relentless love to us. Mediation is downwards. It is we, not God, who are hard to reach."

In the twelfth century Abelard took a different point of view than had Anselm, described as follows by Joseph Campbell: "Jesus' death on the cross was not as ransom paid, or as a penalty applied, but an act of atonement, at-one-ment, with the race." By becoming "at one" with the suffering of life, Jesus evokes the human sentiment of compassion. His cross invites us to focus our hearts on compassionately living for one another.

Is God a Prosecuting Attorney or a Defense Attorney?

Question: I grew up with a God who seemed more like a prosecuting attorney. How did I get that idea, if God is really like a defense attorney?

In classical Greek, long before the New Testament writings appeared, *parakletos* meant "one called alongside" and was used in a legal sense to refer to a defense attorney. Some English translations use the word "advocate" to focus on this aspect of its meaning. The concept of God as defense attorney was primary in the early church, where love and justice were intermingled as two sides of God's mercy. Beginning with Tertullian and Augustine, under the influence of the Roman judicial system, law and obedience were emphasized in such a way that justice was divorced from love. As Deak writes, sin was no longer seen as "a weakening of the bond of love between God and man, but rather as an infringement of the rights of God." Sin came to be seen as a crime, which implied legal vindication through retributive justice. Thus, God became a prosecuting attorney who was no longer bound by the commandment to "love your enemies" and on whom it was very easy to project unhealed human instincts for cruelty and revenge. According to Berdyaev, "religious beliefs have reflected the fallen state of man and the way in which the relations between God and man were conceived has readily taken the form of a criminal trial . . . lawful or legal love is love that has died."

Misuse of the sacrament of reconciliation has reinforced our image of God as a prosecuting attorney. As James Burtchaell says, confession has sometimes

> ... been turned into something reminiscent of a tribunal: the priest sitting in judgment on the failures of the penitent and assigning a token penalty. This is a grotesque confusion, because it embodies precisely what Christians believe God does not do. A judge can never forgive. A judge can only condemn, or acquit. The one thing Jesus can never do on the Father's behalf is punish. The dynamics of a criminal court are perhaps least apt to serve as a suggestion of what God is trying to do to us by his forgiveness.

Question: You say that God forgives and heals the unrepentant sinner. In the story of the prodigal son, doesn't the son first have to repent and go home before the father forgives him?

Although the story of the prodigal son in Luke 15:11–30 is often given as an example of repentance, it is actually a story of how God forgives and heals the unrepentant sinner. This story is Jesus' answer to the Pharisees who ask why he welcomes tax collectors or other unrepentant sinners, and even eats with them (Lk. 15:1–3). Jesus portrays the prodigal as the greatest possible sinner. He committed what to the Jews was the worst possible crime, to treat the father of the family as if he were dead. It was inconceivable for any Jew to ask for his father's inheritance while his father was still healthy (let alone spend that inheritance in a Gentile, pagan land). As Kenneth Bailey writes, "In all of Middle Eastern literature (aside from the prodigal story) from ancient times to the present, there is no case of any son, older or younger, asking for his inheritance from a father who is still in good health."

This story is sometimes read as if the prodigal had a change of heart while in the "far country," and planned to ask his father to make him a "hired servant" as a gesture of repentance. Scripture scholarship, however, indicates that the prodigal's motive at this point is more likely self-interest. Although the words of his prepared speech sound like repentance, he composes them after observing that he would get a lot more to eat if he were back in his father's house. James Burtchaell writes,

> The ruined and desperate son heads home not because he is repentant but because he is starving. The story never suggests that he has had a change of heart; only a change of diet. He is still the same schlemiel [yiddish equivalent of "jerk"] of a son who comes scuffing up the road to the homestead.

The son regrets that he has lost all the money he got from his father, but it is unlikely that he has yet repented of breaking his father's heart.

Another indication of the prodigal's lack of repentance is found in Luke 15:20. While the son "was still a long way off," the father saw him and ran out to greet him. In a personal conversation, scripture scholar Kenneth Bailey told us that the words "while still a long way off" are not meant to indicate the son's geographic distance from the father, but rather his emotional distance, i.e., the son's hardhearted lack of repentance.

The father offers reconciliation to his son before the prodigal has truly repented and without even first asking for a change of heart. According to Bailey, later the father will forgive the elder son before the elder son repents. By arguing with his father in public, the elder son puts a break in the relationship "with his father that is nearly as radical as the break between the father and the younger son at the beginning of the parable." Yet the father will love the unrepentant elder brother and promise that, even if he doesn't come to the banquet, "Everything I have is yours."

Question: The idea that God loves and heals unrepentant sinners, such as the prodigal, is still new to me. Can you give me more evidence from scripture?

The prodigal son is only one of three parables in Luke 15 about how God loves the unrepentant sinner. The parable of the lost prodigal son is preceded by the parable of the lost sheep (Lk. 15:3-7) and the parable of the lost coin (Lk. 15:8-11). Like the lost son, the lost sheep and the lost coin represent the unrepentant sinner. In each of the three parables,

God takes the initiative to seek out what is still lost and unrepentant, rather than waiting for the lost one to repent and come back.

God's willingness to seek out the lost one is significant for all the "found ones" (or those who think they're found) as well. Writing on the parable of the lost sheep, Bailey says, "it is the shepherd's willingness to go after the one that gives the ninety-nine their real security." In the same way, God's willingness to keep seeking out the unrepentant sinner assures all the rest of us that God will never let go of us and allows us to rest secure in that love.

This acceptance of the unrepentant sinner is echoed many other times in the New Testament and it will continue to scandalize the Pharisees. For example:

> Love your enemies and pray for those who persecute you, so that you may be children of your Father in heaven; for he makes his sun rise on the evil and on the good, and sends rain on the righteous and on the unrighteous. For if you love those who love you, what reward do you have. Do not even the tax collectors do the same (Mt. 5:44-46)?

> Indeed, rarely will anyone die for a righteous person—though perhaps for a good person someone might actually dare to die. But God proves his love for us in that while we still were sinners Christ died for us (Rom. 5:7-8).

Question: To me repentance means a change of heart. How can God or anyone else help people who don't want to change? For example, isn't it true that alcoholics can't recover until they "hit bottom" and ask for help?

The 12 Step recovery movement's attitude toward "hitting bottom" and "doing an intervention" has evolved. In the early days of Alcoholics Anonymous, it was often thought that until an alcoholic "hit bottom" and was ready for help, there was little that could be done for that person. According to Dr. Robert Stuckey, today early interventions are encouraged, on people who seemingly don't want help and "show no signs of wanting to reform." If 12 Step group members can break through to people who seemingly don't want to change, so can God.

Question: Are you really saying that God loves and heals us as unrepentant sinners, without us doing anything to earn it, not even asking for help?

Yes. That God loves and heals the unrepentant sinner might seem strange to many of us raised in the "Deuteronomic Code mentality." According to Richard Rohr, the Deuteronomic Code, exemplified by the Ten Commandments, was based on punishing (not healing) the unrepentant sinner. Thus the Deuteronomic Code had the following movement: I sin, God punishes me, I repent, God loves and rewards me. In such a movement, I *earn* God's love and my reward through repentance. But stories such as Paul's conversion or the return of the unrepentant prodigal son turn the Deuteronomic Code upside down. They have a different movement: I sin, I am unrepentant, I am loved and rewarded by God, this heals me so I can repent. In such stories I do not earn God's love and reward through repentance. Instead, "grace" or God's love and reward is *unearned,* a free gift which heals me and makes my eventual repentance possible.

This radical break with the Deuteronomic Code was the hallmark of the covenant introduced by the prophets. In this covenant, God's *mercy* would no longer be in contrast to God's retributive *justice.* Rather, the concepts of mercy and justice are used together. Justice for God now means God being true to Godself as the merciful one, the magnanimous one, the unconditional lover. God would never again vengefully punish sin (Is. 54:9) but rather would heal the hard-hearted by being excessive to the excessive degree, by "astounding this people with prodigies and wonders" (Is. 29:14, Jerusalem Bible).

With this covenant understanding, see if you can pick the proper translation of Luke 7:47. That passage is Jesus' defense of the woman who as a public sinner scandalizes Simon the Pharisee by washing Jesus' feet with her tears and drying them with her hair (Lk. 7:36–50). Jesus' defense of the woman in 7:47 is translated two different ways:

> For this reason I tell you that her sins, her many sins, must have been forgiven her, or she would not have shown such great love. It is the man who is forgiven little who shows little love (Jerusalem Bible).

or

> I tell you that is why her many sins are forgiven—because of her great love. Little is forgiven the one whose love is small (New American Bible).

Which is right? The Jerusalem Bible stresses the covenant understanding. The woman's response, i.e., her acting in a healed way by showing great love, is given by Jesus as evidence of the prior, *unearned* gift of God's love and forgiveness. In contrast, the NAB version reflects the Deuteronomic understanding. The woman's repentance and love *earn* God's reward of forgiveness. The answer to which translation is correct comes from Jesus' question to Simon in Luke 7:42, about whether the one forgiven a debt of five hundred or one forgiven a debt of fifty will love more. Simon's answer, that the one forgiven five hundred will love more, emphasizes that love flows from forgiveness as a response (Jerusalem Bible) rather than from a perfectionistic striving to earn forgiveness (NAB). Because nearly every Bible mistranslates this, the Jerusalem Bible adds a footnote:

> Not as usually translated, "her many sins are forgiven her *because* she has shown such great love." The context demands the reverse: she shows so much affection because she has had so many sins forgiven.

The new (1988) Revised New American Bible agrees with the Jerusalem, and now translates this passage in a similar way.

The fact that this passage is so frequently mistranslated may be a sign not only of our Deuteronomic Code mindset but also of how much we believe that God acts on the American ethic that there are no free gifts and that we have to work hard and *earn* whatever we get.

Question: I've heard that some people have near-death experiences in which they have to account for their whole lives. Do these people have anything to teach us about how God judges us?

Besides scripture, near-death experiences support our belief that God judges us in such a way that we know we are unconditionally loved. Since Dr. Raymond Moody's original research, according to John Heaney there has been a growing acceptance that 21 percent to 59 percent of those who return from clinical death remember a near-death experience that is similar, despite varying religious and cultural backgrounds.

During a "life after life" near-death experience, a dying woman may hear her doctor pronounce her dead while feeling herself sucked rapidly through a long, dark tunnel. She then finds herself outside her physical body, looking down on the doctors still trying to resuscitate her. She experiences herself as having a spiritual body which is very different from her physical body, like a floating amorphous cloud that communicates by thought. Relatives and friends who have already died come to meet her and bring her to a "Being of Light" who accepts and loves her more deeply than she has ever experienced. Like a magnet drawn to iron, she is drawn to the personal acceptance and compassion of this dazzling Being of Light. Moody notes that although this is an experience of light, not one person doubted that it was a personal Being of Light.

Shortly after appearing, the Being of Light asks the question, "What have you done with your life to show me?" This question isn't accusing or threatening, but rather is pervaded with total love and acceptance, no matter what the answer. The non-judgmental Being of Light helps the dying person answer the question by presenting a panoramic review that is like a film of the individual's whole life. This review is meant to provoke reflection. The Being seems to know all and is displaying the review so that the dying person can understand two things: how she loved others and how she learned through her experiences and mistakes. Only when a person learns how she has loved, and how she can deepen her love, does the Being ask her if she would like to stay or return to earth. Although many would like to stay in the next world, all who have returned to tell of their experience have finally decided with the Being of Light that they still have a mission to fulfill on earth, such as raising their young children or giving others the total acceptance radiated by the Being of Light.

Those who return from such experiences bring with them a new and enduring desire to love others and to grow in self-knowledge. They also have less fear of death because they no longer fear God's judgment. The judgment they found was the self-judgment experienced when a loving Mother Teresa of Calcutta awakens one to injustice in neglecting the destitute. Dr. Elisabeth Kübler-Ross reports that meeting such a non-judgmental God helps these people to live non-judgmentally. For instance, after a near-death experience a minister could not continue as pastor of his church. He was enveloped in such a total love upon encountering the Being of Light that he could no longer teach condemnation in the way his denomination demanded.

Question: Are near-death experiences always so positive? I've heard about people who say they went to hell during a near-death experience.

A few people, such as attempted suicides, do report distressful near-death experiences which Moody describes as being stuck and unable to approach the Being of Light. The consensus of researchers is that such negative experiences are extremely rare. Moreover, such people tend to be depressed when they "die," i.e., their own inner state is a "hellish" one. They also tend to be scrupulous and guilt-ridden—they are the ones who try too hard to be "good" and who least fit the description of those one might expect to find in hell. Dr. Kenneth Ring found that if a person has a distressful near-death experience and then "dies" again, his or her second experience is always a positive one. Dr. Ring attributes this to a change in consciousness, in which those who cannot at first adjust to the highly positive state described by most near-death subjects are able to do so by their second experience. We think the change may also be a result of the healing flowing from the first experience.

According to John Heaney, near-death researchers have ruled out wishful thinking, psychological expectations, hallucinations or dreams, and pharmacological explanations for this transpersonal experience at death. Whatever the explanation, resuscitated people often remember a healing experience with a loving Being of Light who judges them in a way that they know they are unconditionally loved.

This non-judgmental Being of Light is much like the Light that Paul encountered, whose question, "Saul, Saul, why do you persecute me?" helped Paul review and learn from his own life (Acts 9:4).

Does God Send Anyone to Hell?

Question: What do you mean when you say that hell exists as a "possibility"?

We're quoting William Dalton, who says that while an eternal hell is an "*abstract* possibility," given what we know of the loving nature of God we may have real hope that God will actually save everyone.

Along the same lines as Dalton, Karl Barth called the choice of hell an "impossible possibility," because human unbelief becomes entirely ineffective in the face of divine love.

Question: What about saints and other mystics who claim to have seen people burning in the fires of hell?

Just as we cannot take all the images in scripture literally, neither can we take all the images in visions (such as fire and hell) literally. The Church has never done so. Karl Rahner wrote,

> The Church, which invokes its infallibility in the canonization of the saints, has never done so with regard to the damned. We cannot know with certainty if even one human soul does in fact go to hell.

Question: You say we don't know if anyone chooses hell, but as we look around don't we see people who seem to be doing just that?

The choice of hell must be looked at from two viewpoints: the viewpoint of human beings and the viewpoint of God. In the parable of the rich young man, Jesus stresses how differently the possibility of salvation looks from the human viewpoint and from God's. When his disciples ask Jesus how anyone could be saved, Jesus says that from the human viewpoint it is impossible, but from God's viewpoint everything is possible (Mk. 10:27). Piet Schoonenberg, S.J., summarizes this parable when he says, "Hell is a possibility in us, and redemption is a still greater possibility in God."

As John A. T. Robinson puts it, "the ultimate point of view about history is not man's but God's." When Hilda first thought about her unrepentant son committing suicide, she thought of it only from the human viewpoint. She thought that her son would surely go to hell until she saw God reaching out to her son. Then she could consider the question from God's viewpoint. We might compare Hilda's son with Robinson's description of human beings walking down the road which eventually leads to hell:

> Somewhere along the first road, far or near from its beginning, man meets Someone, a figure stooping beneath the weight of the Cross. "Lord, why are you doing this?" each of us sometime or other asks. "For you, to prove that you are greatly loved by God." No man can indefinitely meet such great love, especially in his bitter emptiness and loneliness of self-love, and continue to resist. Man will not lose his choice to resist. He will want, like a feverish thirsting man on a desert, to stretch out to drink this life-giving water.

Question: You sound awfully optimistic. I've been going to church all my life and I've never heard this. Are other people in the Church really saying the same thing?

The optimism we express here is consistent with the consensus of current Roman Catholic theology. As Sachs writes, Rahner (consistent with most Roman Catholic theologians) argues for an "unshakable hope" that in the end all men and women will be healed and will enjoy eternal life. In his farewell speech at Freiburg in 1984, Rahner expressed this hope:

> For me, the history of humanity, despite all the disastrous things which have happened to men, even Auschwitz and all the catastrophes which perhaps we must still fear as a result of the exhaustion of all natural resources and nuclear madness, is a history of salvation, a universal history of the power of grace and divine love, a history in which we can hope for all human beings and not just a few.

Deak agrees that Roman Catholic theology is increasingly open to the possibility that all will be saved, and he finds the same movement in Protestant theology as well.

Question: You seem to be arguing for universalism. Isn't that a heresy that was condemned by the Church?

It is important to distinguish between the doctrine of *apokatastasis* (universal restoration), which says that all *must* be saved, and universalism, which says that all *will* be saved. As Deak writes,

> The *doctrine* of *apokatastasis* assumes that some day the entire creation will be brought home to God in full eschatalogical harmony and peace; whereas universalism, though believing the same, refrains from advocating it as a necessity.

The critical difference is that *apokatastasis* seems to eliminate free will entirely, while universalism preserves it but assumes that all people will eventually use their free will to choose God. To summarize the idea of universalism, Deak writes,

> God not only *wants* all to be saved, but He will *in reality* effect this through the free cooperation of man, so that when time runs out and gives place to eternity, He will be indeed all in all (Eph. 1:10; Col. 1:20).

One objection that is sometimes raised to the idea of universal salvation is the belief that Origen (born in 186 A.D.) was condemned for it. However, it appears that Origen was condemned at the Synod of Constantinople in 543 for *apokatastasis* and for his theory of salvation history as returning aeons rather than as uni-linear. According to Deak and Dalton, evidence in support of this is that Gregory of Nyssa (380 A.D.) who was a strong proponent of universalism, but who rejected the idea of returning aeons, was never condemned by any council. Paul Smith lists other early universalists who were not condemned, such as Clement of Alexandria (190 A.D., head of the catechetical school there), Hilary (deacon of the Roman Church), Titus, Bishop of Bostra (364 A.D.),

Gregory of Nazianzus (373 A.D., president of the second great Ecumenical Council), and Jerome (346 A.D., translator of the Latin Bible).

Question: You give scripture passages by St. Paul that sound universalist, but doesn't he also have some harsh things to say about those who turn away from God?

Paul certainly does emphasize the seriousness of turning away from God and the condemnation this warrants (e.g., Rom. 2:5-8; 1 Cor. 6:9-10; 2 Cor. 5:10; 2 Thess. 1:5-9; Phil. 3:19). However, he never affirms that any human being, given the love and mercy of God, actually does turn away permanently. In other words, his statements may be taken as warnings, not as descriptions of actual future events. Dalton writes that overall, in Paul's thinking, "human sin is seen as explicable only as a stage on the way towards the triumph of God's grace." Thus Paul can say, "God has imprisoned all in disobedience so that he may be merciful to all" (Rom. 11:32).

Question: You claim Jesus never said that anyone is in hell. What about Jesus' story of Lazarus and Dives, in Luke 16:19-31?

Jesus' story of the rich man (Dives) and Lazarus (a poor beggar) is sometimes cited to prove that there *are* people in hell, or that once a person gets to hell he or she cannot leave. Lazarus, a poor beggar, dies and goes to heaven where he is in the bosom of Abraham. Dives, who had not reached out to help Lazarus, dies and goes to hell. Dives asks if he can go back and warn his five brothers so that they will not end up in hell too. Abraham refuses.

A clue that this story is not to be taken literally as proof that some people are in an eternal state of hell is Dives' desire to help others and Abraham's refusal to permit it. If we define heaven as a state of giving and receiving love, and hell as a state of total alienation in which no love is given or received and repentance is impossible, then the compassionate, unselfish, repentant Dives is at this point behaving more like a resident of heaven than is Abraham. What the story does seem to be saying is two things. First, social standing in this world can be turned upside down in the next. Secondly, if you ignore your brothers and sisters in need (as Dives did previously), you will feel like hell.

Dalton discusses this and the other New Testament passages that are most commonly cited to prove that there are people in hell. However, as he points out, it is not ultimately helpful to argue one passage against another. Fundamental theological issues, such as human salvation, must be understood, not on the basis of individual texts, but in light of the core message of the gospel.

Question: Does the idea that we make a final decision for or against God at the moment of death have any basis in scripture?

Deak argues that there is no conclusive biblical evidence for fixing the moment of ultimate choice in the last conscious moment before death. He believes the idea originated for pastoral reasons, such as "to provide an incentive to use the present according to one's best knowledge for building up a sound God-man relationship; or to provide a deterrent against putting off an existential decision for or against accepting God in faith." While these reasons may have some pastoral usefulness, that doesn't mean the underlying idea regarding our last conscious moment is true.

Although the Roman Catholic tradition believes that after death we cannot change our basic orientation for or against God, Bulgakov explains that the Eastern Orthodox tradition holds that conversion can take place after death, until the last judgment. Robinson offers support for this tradition when he writes, "The New Testament never dogmatizes to the extent of saying that after death there is no further chance."

Question: The idea that God spends God's eternity loving and healing us is new to me. Do theologians support your viewpoint?

Many theologians question the idea of a final, definitive decision at death which would rule out God's ongoing healing initiatives. For example, Hans Küng writes,

Definitive? Do not the psalms say that God rules over the realm of the dead? What is supposed to become definitive here, contrary to the will of an all-merciful and almighty God? Why should God, who is infinitely good, want to perpetuate enmity instead of removing it and in practice to share his rule forever with some kind of anti-God? Why should he have nothing more to say at this point and consequently render forever impossible a purification, cleansing, liberation, enlightenment, of guilt-laden man?

Like Küng, Berdyaev challenged the contradiction of traditional Christian doctrine, in which "freedom which leads to *hell* is recognized, but freedom which leads *out of it* is denied."

When we speak of "the moment of death," what we usually mean is the last conscious moment *before* death. This would be a moment of limited freedom, since we still carry all the hurts we have experienced in this world and since we have not yet experienced all God's healing initiatives. Ladislaus Boros suggests that in death itself there is a moment of perfect freedom when we are no longer bound by the hurts and limitations of this world, in which we choose our final destiny. In this moment,

> No one is damned because he was born into a family in which he never experienced love and, therefore, could not also understand what the nature of God is. No one is damned because he probably turned against a God in whom he saw only a God of commandments, a terrible tyrant. No one is damned because he was despised, detested, misjudged and inwardly hurt and so revolted against everything, even against God.

Boros' conception of this moment in death corresponds to our idea of a moment in which, in order to be perfectly free, we would have to experience a whole eternity of God's healing initiatives.

Question: Is there anything in scripture to support your idea that God spends eternity loving and healing us?

The prodigal story provides an image of how God spends God's eternity trying to love and heal. That Hilda imagined herself embracing her deceased unrepentant son in the same way the Father embraced the unrepentant prodigal is not a surprise. The story of the prodigal is the Gospel of Luke's answer to the same question Hilda asked Dennis: What would happen if my son would die without repenting? The story of the prodigal is not only about how God relates in everyday life to unrepentant sinners but also about afterlife's messianic banquet thrown by God for an unrepentant son "who was dead and has come back to life" (Lk. 15:24, 32). Joachim Jeremias describes the parable of the prodigal son in terms of the eschatalogical meal in which "the end-time brings with it a reversal of conditions. In this reversal, salvation comes to the sinner, not the righteous."

Luke's Gospel has five consecutive chapters dealing with afterlife, one of which is Chapter 15. A hint that the banquet celebrations in the parables of the lost sheep, the lost coin and the lost son are afterlife banquets is given by the word *prosdechomai* (welcome). According to Charles Giblin, this word is consistently associated in the New Testament with afterlife themes such as the coming of the kingdom or parousia. Luke uses this afterlife word to introduce the three parables in Chapter 15 about unrepentant sinners. In each parable, what is lost (sheep, coin, son) represents the lost and unrepentant sinner. All three parables celebrate how even in afterlife, love compels God to search out and find the lost, unrepentant sinners. The joyful heavenly banquet in each story celebrates how the compelling love of God, that searched out these unrepentant sinners, made their repentance possible.

What About the Hell of Suffering?

Question: Can you say more about how hurts affect our image of God?

In this book we are focusing on the damage to our image of God caused by teaching that distorts Jesus' message of love. In writing about his experience in the concentration camp, Elie Wiesel refers to the damage to our image of God that can come from experiences of tragedy and suffering. At such times God may seem to have abandoned us or (even worse) to have caused the evil we experience. Every hurt can affect our image of God, and the more serious the hurt the more profoundly it may distort our image of God. Thus, for example, abuse victims may have great difficulty trusting God, and atheists can often trace their loss of faith to the loss of a loved one.

I (Matt) lost my two-year-old brother, John, when I was seven. I was told that God "took" John, and I was not encouraged to grieve. My image of God was seriously affected for many years, until I completed the grieving process. Healing involves resolving grief and discovering that God has been present all along in the depth of our pain, suffering with us. As Pierre Wolf writes, our anger at suffering is God's anger.

Our image of God is also affected by lack of bonding with primary caregivers (as well as the abusive child-rearing practices mentioned above). Our other books and our tapes deal with the healing of hurts, such as death, loss and lack of adequate bonding. They are listed in Resources for Further Growth.

What About Free Will?

Question: Are you saying that whenever I choose something that is not good, I am not free?

In English, "freedom" must be distinguished from "choice." It is true that we can choose good or evil, but freedom is only toward the greatest good—not only toward what is better, but toward what is *best.* As Augustine put it, "The ability to sin is not the use of freedom, but the abuse of freedom." Karl Barth agreed. He wrote,

> Is it freedom to decide for the devil? The only freedom that means something is freedom to be myself as I am created by God. God did not create a neutral creature, but *His* creature. . . . Being a slave of Christ means being free.

♦ 73

Question: I was taught that mortal sin requires full consent of the will. Are you saying there is no such thing as mortal sin?

The traditional formulation for mortal sin is "serious matter, sufficient reflection, and full consent of the will." Full consent of the will clearly suggests a free and responsible decision to do what is evil. We question whether anyone ever makes such a decision. The position we are taking here, consistent with Rahner and others, is expressed by James Burtchaell:

> As for full consent: no one ever fully consents to evil. We enter evil without much consent, and by entering it we impair our faculty of consent....
>
> Our mistake is to look for responsibility as the hallmark of sin. Ministers of criminal law want to know the extent to which a suspect really entered responsibly into a crime. This is foolish because criminal behavior is not the result of responsible actions; it arises from the extinction of responsibility. So with sin.
>
> Serious matter, sufficient reflection, full consent: that's a description of virtue, not of vice.

Tony deMello, S.J., frequently said something similar during his retreats: that we cannot sin when we are fully aware. Like the prodigal son, when we "come to our senses at last," we choose the good (Lk. 15:17).

Carl Rogers and his colleagues observed this with their clients in psychotherapy. As the unconditional positive regard of the therapist empowered the client to reconnect with aspects of the self that had been lost to awareness,

> The person comes to *be* what he *is,* as clients so frequently say in therapy. What this seems to mean is that the individual comes to *be*—in awareness—what he *is*—in experience. He is, in other words, a complete and fully functioning human organism.
>
> ... when man is less than fully man—when he denies to awareness various aspects of his experience—then indeed we have all too often reason to fear him and his behavior, as the present world situation testifies. But when he is most fully man, when he is his

complete organism, when awareness of experience, that peculiarly human attribute, is most fully operating, then he is to be trusted, then his behavior is constructive.

Along these same lines, Daniel J. O'Hanlon, S.J., writes,

> ...it is possible to allow love to simply emerge out of awareness, without making its cultivation the first object of concern.... In the East great attention is paid to awareness, free of clinging to what is there or trying to get rid of it. More attention is given to this simple awareness, this bare immediate attention, than to the direct cultivation or excitation of feelings and desires. This practice seems to spring out of the conviction that love and compassion are the natural movement of our true self. When the surface mind and disordered desires are still, the true self awakens without need of any further assistance from us. Indeed, our clumsy efforts to poke at it and deliberately rouse it often have the same effect as poking at a sea anemone. It simply closes up tight. But give it stillness, leave it undisturbed, and it opens wide like a water lily in full bloom.

Jesus, who was the only perfectly aware person, was therefore also the only perfectly free person. Jesus always chose the good. The more we become like Jesus, the more we approximate his perfect freedom, and the more we, too, can only choose the good. Similarly, Christian theology has always regarded the deceased in heaven as unable to sin. Alluding to Barth's description of the choice of hell as an "impossible possibility," Deak writes that "though the blessed ones have all the freedom to sin (i.e., it is 'possible'), precisely because of their freedom and knowledge of God they are unable to do so (i.e., it is 'impossible')."

Question: You say that a perfectly free person cannot say "No"' to God. What about Adam and Eve, or the fallen angels? Weren't they perfectly free and didn't they say "No" to God?

Sometimes the story of Adam and Eve in Genesis 2:5–3:24 is put forth as historical evidence that a perfectly free person can say "No" to God. Following St. Irenaeus, we want to suggest an alternative interpretation of this story, in which Adam and Eve were not perfectly free in any mature sense. Rather, the story symbolizes every person's journey toward authentic freedom by moving from unconsciousness to consciousness.

The story of the fallen angels has elements similar to the story of Adam and Eve. Scripture scholars generally agree that neither story is to be taken literally as an historical event, and there is evidence that the basis for the story of the fallen angels does not come from the Bible. One account of the fall of the angels is the heavenly battle presented in the intertestamental book of Enoch, a book not included in the canonical Bible. The other basis for the story of the fallen angels is probably a misinterpretation of Genesis 6:1-4, where the "sons of God" were incorrectly thought to be fallen angels who married the "daughters of men." According to The Jerusalem Bible, in the 4th century, theologians re-interpreted Genesis 6:1-4 saying that the sons of God were not fallen angels but rather Seth's descendants, and that the daughters of men were Cain's descendants.

In the New Testament, Jude 1:6 and 2 Peter 2:4 probably based their story of the fallen angels on the mistaken interpretation of Genesis 6:1-4, in which the sons of God were fallen angels. But even so, when Jude and Peter speak of the fallen angels, such angels are imprisoned until the Day of Judgment, thus leaving open the possibility that they may be freed then. *The Jerome Biblical Commentary* on Jude 1:6 adds that "The imprisoned angels awaiting judgment in 2 Peter and Jude are identified by some with the 'spirits in prison' of 1 Peter 3:19," to whom Christ preaches. There is no point in preaching to spirits if they are eternally condemned. The Greek Orthodox Church encourages its believers to pray for the salvation of the fallen angels (including Satan).

"God Is a Father; More Than That, God Is a Mother"

Question: Why are you equating masculinity with outer space and femininity with inner space?

The tendency of men and women to be oriented differently begins at the physiological level. While the male experiences his penis as an instrument for penetration and exploration of a mystery which is essentially outside of himself, the female experiences her womb as an internal center of mystery, capable of receiving and nurturing life. Erik Erikson was one of the first to articulate the consequences of this physiological difference. During a research study in which 300 school-age children were asked to construct a scene using toys and blocks, Erikson noticed that the 150 boys in the study constructed scenes which consistently differed from the scenes constructed by the 150 girls, in ways that paralleled differences in body structure. The boys tended to build high towers and houses with protrusions and to describe scenes full of activity and danger, while the girls tended to build low enclosures with developed interiors, and to describe peaceful scenes. Thus, the boys' scenes emphasized outer space, while the girls' scenes emphasized inner space.

Question: You're saying God is no more male than female. Why then do we use masculine names, "Father" and "Son," for the first and second persons of the Trinity?

Sandra Schneiders explains this well:

No matter how entrenched in the imagination of the average Christian the image of a male God might be, theological tradition has never assigned sex to God. St. Gregory of Nazianzus well represented the tradition when he affirmed that the terms "Father" and "Son" as applied to the persons of the Trinity were not names of natures or essences but of relations and even in this case the terms are used metaphorically. In other words, God is neither a father nor a son but the first person of the Trinity is related to the second person as origin is related to that which is originated. Because the ancients believed that God was indeed personal, and because their defective biology ascribed all agency in procreation or personal originating activity to the male partner, their choice of "father" for the originating person of the Trinity was logical enough. And since they wished to affirm the absolute likeness and equality of the one originated to the divine principle they called the second person the "son." They were, however, quite aware of the metaphorical nature of their language and never intended to impute actual sexuality to the God whom Scripture affirms is pure Spirit (cf. Jn. 4:24).

Question: When Jesus told us to call God "Abba," or "Father," wasn't he encouraging us to think of God as male?

"Abba" means "Daddy" or "Papa." According to Bernard Cooke, for Jesus the use of "Abba" was not meant to reveal God as a *male* person only (as opposed to a female person), but rather as an intimately *parental* person (as opposed to the distant, patriarchal God-image of his day).

Regarding Jesus' use of words like "Abba" and "Father," Sandra Schneiders reminds us of Jesus' continual presentation of himself as "the sent one," as "a son who is gradually initiated into his father's trade, apprenticed to his father until such time as he is able to take over the 'family business,'" i.e., to save the world. She writes,

> In the patriarchal culture of Jesus a mother-son relationship could not have carried this meaning because mothers had no independent trades and they did not train their male children for adult work. The cultural constraints under which the mystery of redemptive incarnation took place demanded that Jesus experience himself as son of a divine father in order to describe the unique revelation of which he was the subject.... Jesus certainly did not experience God or think of God as exclusively masculine or he could not have presented God in feminine metaphors.

In fact, despite the constraints of his culture, Jesus did sometimes use feminine metaphors to describe God. For example, in Luke, Jesus tells three parables of the merciful forgiveness of God, and in the second one he presents God as the woman householder who searches for a lost coin (Lk. 15:8–10; see also Mt. 23:37, 13:33). In speaking of God as feminine and maternal, Jesus was drawing on the Old Testament. For instance, Isaiah speaks of God as a loving mother in labor and the author of the Book of Numbers speaks of God as one who gives birth, breastfeeds, and carries the child in her bosom (Num. 11:12; see also Ex. 34:6, Dt. 32:18, Is. 49:15, 63:15, 66:13 and Ps. 131:2).

Question: I was taught that Mary is our mother, and I pray to her all the time. Why do I need God the Mother?

With all respect to Mary, she doesn't solve the problem. Mary is commonly presented as a very special human being, but human nevertheless and therefore subordinate to God. Thus, she does not correct the imbalance in Christian spirituality, in which the feminine is subordinate to the masculine.

Question: When you speak of rahamim, *are you saying that the only loving side of God is the feminine side?*

Not at all. John Paul II speaks of the divine mercy of God as having two aspects, described by two Hebrew words, *rahamim* and *hesed.* They suggest two different ways of loving. *Hesed* means God's fidelity, the fatherly love of God, in which God is faithful to his promises because he is faithful to himself. *Rahamim* means God's tender compassion, the motherly love of God which never rejects the child of her womb.

Question: I've never before heard your idea of the masculine emphasis on God's transcendence and the feminine emphasis on God's immanence. Does anyone else support what you say?

The idea that the masculine emphasis on outer space encourages a perception of God as transcendent, while the feminine emphasis on inner space encourages a perception of God as immanent, first came to us from Erikson. James Nelson says something similar:

> While the woman tends to experience her sexuality as more internal and mysterious, a man is inclined to experience his sexual body not as that which possesses mystery but more as an instrument for penetrating and exploring the mystery which is essentially external to himself.
>
> . . . these bodily experiences appear to incline men toward certain spiritual contours. One is externality. Mystery is less within than

"out there." Mystery, which thus lies beyond the self, is to be penetrated by a self which is demarked by specific boundaries. Mystery is to be explored and, if need be, conquered. So it is with God, the ultimate mystery. God is experienced more as transcendent than immanent, more beyond than within. Such, characteristically, has been the shape of a male-dominated theology. . . . Orientation to mystery is more one of penetrating otherness than of embracing it within. The mood is one of conquest, analysis, distinction, understanding. And the mystery itself is likely to be understood as dominantly characterized by stereotypically masculine virtues: order, structure, law and rationality.

Joseph Campbell writes that, "in religions where the god or creator is the mother, the whole world is her body. There is nowhere else. The male god is usually somewhere else."

Question: You've spoken of how men and women tend to perceive God differently. Does that mean they also tend to perceive the whole process of salvation differently?

It seems to us that another aspect of ascribing skewed male values to God is the perception of ourselves being saved as autonomous individuals, rather than as interconnected members of a community. As Carol Gilligan, Joann Conn and many others have pointed out, the masculine emphasis is toward autonomy and the feminine emphasis is toward interconnectedness.

The traditional understanding of hell has stressed the masculine emphasis, in that each person is seen as making a separate, autonomous choice of heaven or hell. The limitation of this point of view became clear to me (Sheila) when my mother died. My mother had not been a loving person during her life; she was the sort of person who some might have thought would end up in hell. During her life, I often prayed for her by simply sending love into her. I never felt anything coming back to me. After she died, for the first time I felt her loving me in return, through the communion of saints. I knew that she was with God, and being healed. Although I had been loved by a grandmother, aunts and female teachers, the quality of my own mother's love, which I had never known before, was unique. This was extremely healing for me, and critical for my development. It was evident to me that if my mother had been forever lost in hell, a part of me would have been forever lost as well. The feminine insight that we are all interconnected suggests that we are all saved or lost together.

Robinson comes to a similar conclusion, from the Hebrew understanding of the body not as the symbol of our individuality, but rather of our solidarity with all of creation. Thus, the doctrine of the resurrection of the body is,

> ... an assertion that no individual can be saved apart from the whole. Through his body he is organically linked with all other life and all other matter in the universe. There is no redemption for the individual *out* of this mass, but only in it and with it. The Christian gospel is not of the rescuing of individuals out of nature and history... but the redeeming of all the myriad relationships of creation into a new heaven and a new earth, the city of God, the body of Christ (see Rom. 8:19-23; Phil. 3:21; etc.).

Dalton also makes the point that we are saved or lost together. He emphasizes our co-responsibility for another's failures, through our own failures of love:

> ... if any of my brothers ends up in an eternal hell, can I be truly saved? ... every sin of mine adds to the contagion of the world's sin. This goes far beyond bad example or personal influence. We are all partly responsible for the future sins of other men.

Question: Are you saying I can't be a mature person if I have an all-male God?

We don't want to judge who is a mature person. However, psychosexual maturity does seem to us more difficult to achieve for those with an all-male God, because we become like the God we adore. For example, Joann Conn observed among her women students that those who "'don't mind that God is pictured only as a man or that we aren't allowed to do the same things men do in the Church'" are constricted in their personal development, whereas those who are developing in their identity experience a strain in their relationship with God if their God image does not include femininity. Thus, if a woman does not see a continuity between her developing identity—her nature as a mature woman—and the nature of God, she will either abandon her own deepest identity or abandon (or at least revise) her belief in God.

So, too, a man without a feminine image of God may live his life out of touch with his own feminine side. Or, he may have to abandon belief in God as a principal source of growth as he seeks to discover his feminine side in another way. According to Andrew Greeley, men whose image of God does include the feminine are more balanced in their personalities and more spiritually mature, tend to have better relationships with women, and are more committed to social justice.

Question: A deep hurt that many women in our culture suffer is sexual abuse. Would changing our image of God affect that?

We think so. It seems that a symptom of the devaluation of women in our culture and church is the high incidence of rape in the United States. In contrast, Peggy Sanday found that there is little or no rape in cultures which have a feminine image of God and where women take an active role in religious ritual.

Why Is It So Important To Change Our Image of God?

Question: Can you give me some examples of how violence toward others is related to our image of God?

We've already mentioned capital punishment, which we believe is related to the vengeful image of God held by so many people in our country. Despite the fact that innocent people have been executed, a June, 1991, Gallup Poll reported in *NCR* found that 76 percent of all Americans and 77 percent of Catholics favored the death penalty for convicted murderers (although the U.S. Catholic bishops and most leaders of religious orders oppose the death penalty). The words of Hans-Jürgen Verweyen, quoted by John Sachs, seem to apply:

Whoever reckons with the possibility of even only *one* person's being lost besides himself is hardly able to love unreservedly. . . . Just the slightest nagging thought of a final hell for others tempts us, in moments in which human togetherness becomes especially difficult, to leave the other to himself.

Another example would be some of the wars we have fought with "God on our side." For decades our country has sung the "Battle Hymn of the Republic," which celebrates a vengeful God sitting on "his judgment seat" striking enemies with "his terrible swift sword." We have sung this song to justify wars with Native American Indians or with other countries, in which our country has acted as vengefully as the God the song celebrates. Catholic theologians Thomas and Gertrude Sartory write of the relationship between Christianity's belief in hell and its involvement in mass murder:

> No religion in the world (not a single one in the history of humanity) has on its conscience so many millions of people who thought differently, believed differently. Christianity is the most murderous religion there has ever been. Christians today have to live with this, they have to "overcome" this sort of past. . . . If someone is convinced that God condemns a person to hell for all eternity for no other reason than because he is a heathen, a Jew, or a heretic, he cannot for his own part fail to regard all heathens, Jews and heretics as good for nothing, as unfit to exist and unworthy of life. Seen from this viewpoint, the almost complete extermination of the North and South American Indians by the "Christian" conquerors is quite consistent. From the aspect of the dogma of hell "baptism or death" is an understandable motto.

Does Fear of Hell Cause Addiction and Negative Behaviors?

Question: You say the feeling of not belonging (to God, ourselves, others and the universe) underlies every addiction. What about genetic factors?

By emphasizing the need for belonging we do not mean to overlook the role of genetic predisposition in addiction. Our understanding is that a genetic predisposition affects which addiction we choose (e.g., alcoholism, overeating, pedophilia, etc.), but that addiction itself is an attempt to handle unresolved inner pain. In other words, if I am filled with shame and loneliness, and do not know how to process my feelings in a healthy way that enables me to give and receive love, depending upon my genetic predisposition, I may drink, eat, molest children, etc. to avoid my inner pain. The importance of belonging, in addictions and recovery, is explored in our book *Belonging: Bonds of Healing & Recovery.*

Question: Besides addictions, how is the fear of hell related to emotional illness in general?

A therapist who has small children told us, "If I want to correct my children, I must first establish an atmosphere in which they know that I will never abandon them." Our friend understands that the fear of abandonment and not belonging, based on the belief that we are loved only on condition that we are "good," underlies not only addictions but most, if not all, emotional illness. We first learn this fear with our human parents and then we are likely to project it onto God. The great Swiss psychiatrist Paul Tournier writes, "Fear of losing the love of God— this is the essence of our human problem and of psychology." As Bernard Cooke says, psychological health demands that we know God is

> ...absolutely faithful and unswerving in a compassionate love of us humans. God does not go from being displeased with us to being once more friendly; God is infinitely above being offended and does not ask to be appeased. God's forgiveness is not a response to our admission of guilt and our conversion; it is their cause.
>
> In some ways a loving parent's way of dealing with a child gives us an insight into the divine attitude toward human sin: while the parent will lead the young person to recognition of misdeeds and at a certain age to a sense of culpability, while the parent will work to help the child change to a better attitude and a better pattern of behavior, the parent's forgiveness of the child does not wait for some appeal for that forgiveness. Instead, the forgiveness is assumed even before the child's "sin." It is never retracted at any point and is a per-

sonal force that energizes the parent's effort to lead the child toward moral responsibility.

Punishment Never Heals, Only Love Can Heal

Question: If the fear of punishment can never change a person, why does the Bible tell us to fear God?

Some justify the use of fear to control others' behavior by saying that the scriptures tell us to "fear God." However, the word we translate as "fear," in expressions like "fear of the Lord" (*phobos*), is not the experience of being intimidated by another. According to William Barclay, *phobos*, in relation to God, would better be translated "awesome respect," meaning loving wonder (e.g., Ps. 103:11-17).

We Are All Good Goats

Question: Matthew 25 is the passage I've most often heard quoted to prove that some people go to heaven and some people go to hell. Can you give me any more evidence for your interpretation?

Deak's interpretation of Matthew 25:31-46 is similar to ours. He says that sheep and goats represent not two different groups of persons, but two realities that coexist within every person, "realized goodness" and "past failures."

We recognize that this way of understanding Matthew 25 does not exhaust the meaning of the passage. We cannot deny the historical dimension, the "not-yet," of revelation, and say that the kingdom of God is *only* within us in our present experience. However, we can say that it is *also* within us in our present experience. Thus our present inner experience is essential information for our effort to understand the mysteries of heaven and hell.

On the other hand, Dalton does take the passage in the more historical sense, as referring to two groups of persons. He sees the message to the goats as a warning, not as a statement of what will actually happen. Referring to the situation of the goats, he says, "it is not affirmed that any human being, given the grace and mercy of God, ever arrives at this desperate situation."

The great scripture scholar William Barclay described himself as a "convinced universalist." Commenting on Matthew 25:46, in which the goats on the left hand are sent away to "eternal punishment," he says that what is meant is not damnation that lasts forever. Rather, what is meant is the remedial, healing action of God that takes place in a realm that is different from our concept of time:

> The Greek word for punishment is *kolasis*, which was not originally an ethical word at all. It originally meant the pruning of trees to make them grow better. I think it is true to say that in all Greek secular literature, *kolasis* is never used of anything but remedial punishment. The word for eternal is *aiónios*. It means more than everlasting, for Plato—who may have invented the word—plainly says that a thing may be everlasting and still not be *aiónios*. A simple way to put it is that *aiónios* cannot be used properly of anyone but God; it is the word uniquely, as Plato saw it, of God. Eternal punishment is then literally that kind of remedial punishment which it befits God to give and which only God can give.

Question: When you interpret the scriptures about hell symbolically, aren't you distorting the Church's teaching?

We believe the real distortion has come from taking literally and for all time what was intended to be taken symbolically in a particular time—what Rosemary Radford Reuther calls "the tyranny of the absolutizing imagination." Paul Tillich wrote,

> The first step toward non-religion of the Western world was made by religion itself. This was when it defended its great symbols, which were its means of interpreting the world and life, not as symbols, but as literal stories.

Karl Rahner and other theologians suggest that what the Church needs today is a reformulation of Church dogma concerning hell. This reformulation of dogma is especially critical because many of the official statements of the teaching Church are based on the literal interpretations of such scriptural words as "fire," "everlasting," and "hell," whereas Jesus intended a symbolic interpretation. William Dalton gives the following example:

> In the first Ecumenical Council of Lyons we are required to believe that the damned 'are forever tortured in the fires of everlasting gehenna' (Dz 839). Whatever the fathers of the council thought, their words today are misleading, even erroneous, if they are not interpreted symbolically.

Question: You've said that language about heaven and hell should be understood symbolically. How then do I understand words like "the everlasting fire of hell"?

When Jesus speaks about the "everlasting fire of hell" he is using an image to describe the chaos of a person headed in a self-destructive direction. The word we translate as "hell" comes from the Hebrew *gehenna*. Gehenna was a valley in southeastern Jerusalem, used as a garbage dump. The garbage was burned, and the geography of the valley created a constant current of air which had kept the dump blazing continually for generations before Jesus' time. The visual message of gehenna or hell was, "If you don't take care of yourself, you're going to deteriorate just like the garbage." To Jews, gehenna was part of this world, describing what was happening now. In other words, Jesus is using a contemporary image without judging its theological accuracy and without trying to describe literally a place of future punishment. Rather, as in other places where Jesus speaks about the threat of vindictive punishment, he is not speaking because he intends to send people to hell, but rather to show how important it is to obey so that his disciples can be well themselves and can love each other more.

Thus, for instance, in Matthew 25 Jesus uses such imagery to underline his deep ultimate concern for human values like feeding the hungry, clothing the naked and visiting those in prison. Jesus' apocalyptic images are meant to accurately underline his deep ultimate concern for his followers to love one another, rather than meant to accurately describe future punishment. For example, "fire" does not mean physical flames which God created so that those suffering from the flames might make expiatory payment for their sins. According to Kalistos Ware, fire is an image of God's love which could be present even in hell. As Rahner says,

> The metaphors in which Jesus describes the eternal perdition of man as a possibility which threatens him at this moment are images (fire, worm, darkness) taken from the mental furniture of contemporary apocalyptic literature. . . . Even such a term as 'eternal loss' is in the nature of an image.

"Everlasting" or "eternal" (*aiónios* in Greek) was understood by Jesus as an image that could describe a temporary state. *Aiónios* is an adjective from the Greek noun *aión* which the *Greek-English Lexicon of the New Testament* lists as meaning an indefinite period of time ranging from a "generation" or a person's "lifetime" to "lasting forever." It is likely that for Jesus the image "eternal fire of hell" referred to the indefinite period of time during which the air currents had kept gehenna's garbage dump blazing.

As already mentioned, scripture scholar William Barclay defines *aiónios* as referring to a different *quality* of time (God's time instead of human time), rather than to a quantity of time: "We shall never enter into the full idea of eternal life until we rid ourselves of the almost instinctive assumption that eternal life means primarily life which goes on forever."

George Maloney writes: "Although writings of the Septuagint (such as the Book of Daniel and the Books of Maccabees) use words such as 'forever,' 'eternal,' and 'everlasting,' . . . the meaning is a popular description for an indefinite period of time." Thus "forever" or "everlasting" is an image and in no way is meant to be only "a metaphysical concept of unending, everlasting timelessness as we understand it today."

Perhaps the most important thing to remember is not only that words such as "everlasting" and "forever" are images, but that they are images spoken by a lover. One day to a lover, such as a father searching for his lost prodigal son or lost elder son, could be "forever." After the loss of Dennis and Matt's granddad, their grandmother said that one day seemed longer to her than her previous fifty-two years of marriage. If you have ever waited a few hours for a phone call from someone with whom you needed to be reconciled, you know that those few hours can seem like forever.

Sources

Augustine Contra Julianum opus imperfectum, liber 6, XI (PL 45, col. 1519, line 42), trans. by Francis Kelly Nemeck, O.M.I.

Kenneth Bailey, *The Cross and the Prodigal* (St. Louis: Concordia, 1973). Lost sheep, 22.

Kenneth Bailey, *Poet and Peasant and Through Peasant Eyes* (Grand Rapids: Eerdmans, 1976). Woman who washes Jesus' feet, 1-21. Prodigal son, 164, 176-177, 183-184, 195.

William Barclay, *New Testament Words* (Philadelphia: Westminster, 1974). *Phobos,* 227-232. *Aiónios,* 33-41.

William Barclay, *A Spiritual Autobiography* (Grand Rapids: Eerdmans, 1975). Matthew 25, 58-61.

Karl Barth, *Church Dogmatics,* trans. by G. L. M. Haire, et al. (Edinburgh: T & T Clark, 1936), II/2. "Impossible possiblity," 503.

Karl Barth, *Table Talk,* ed. by John D. Godsey (Edinburgh: Oliver and Boyd, 1963). Freedom, 37.

Nikolai Berdyaev, *The Destiny of Man* (New York: Charles Scribner's Sons, 1937). Freedom which leads out of hell, 348.

Nikolai Berdyaev, *Truth and Revelation,* tr. by R.M. French (London: G. Bles, 1953), 114 and *Dream and Reality* (London: G. Bles, 1950), 71. On God and a criminal trial. Both cited in Deak, 22.

Ladislaus Boros, "Regarding the Theology of Death," in *Readings in Christian Eschatology,* ed. by Franz Mussner (Derby, NY: Society of St. Paul, 1966), 124ff.

Raymond E. Brown, *The Gospels and Epistles of John* (Collegeville: Liturgical Press, 1988). *Parakletos,* 80.

Serge Bulgakov, *The Orthodox Church* (London: Centenary Press, 1935), 208-209.

James Tunstead Burtchaell, C.S.C., "An Ancient Gift, a Thing of Joy," *Notre Dame* Magazine (Winter, 1985-86). Prodigal son, 15. Confession as a tribunal, 16. Mortal sin, 18. Downward mediation, 22; also found in *Philemon's Problem: The Daily Dilemma of the Christian* (Chicago: ACTA, 1973).

Joseph Campbell, *The Power of Myth* (New York: Doubleday, 1988). Abelard's salvation theology, 112. God as Mother, 49.

Joann Wolski Conn, "Spirituality and Personal Maturity," in Robert J. Wicks et al. (eds.), *Clinical Handbook of Pastoral Counseling* (New York: Paulist Press, 1985), 37-57. On autonomy vs. connectedness.

Joann Wolski Conn, "Restriction and Reconstruction," in *Women's Spirituality* (Mahwah, NJ: Paulist Press, 1986). Feminine God image, 14-16.

Bernard Cooke, "Forgiving Yourself: The Basis of All Reconciliation," *Praying,* No. 19 (July-August, 1987). God's attitude toward us, 11.

Bernard Cooke, "Non-Patriarchal Salvation," in Joann Wolski Conn (ed.), *Women's Spirituality* (Mahwah, NJ: Paulist Press, 1986) 274-286. On Jesus calling God "Abba."

William J. Dalton, S.J., *Salvation and Damnation* (Theology Today Series, #41) (Butler, WI: Clergy Book Service, 1977). Study of the scripture passages most often used to argue that there are people in hell. Origen, 75-76. Luke 16:19-31, 37. Matthew 25, 40. Human sin in St. Paul, 44. Co-responsibility, 73. Symbolic language, 17-73, 80.

Esteban Deak, *Apokatastasis: The Problem of Universal Salvation in Twentieth Century Theology* (Esteban Deak: Toronto, 1979, ISBN #0969011504). Summary of Protestant and Roman Catholic thinking about universal salvation. God as prosecuting attorney, 22, 33-38, 284-285, 307-315, 359. Barth's view of hell as "impossible possibility," 278, 346. Protestant theology moving in direction of universalism, 208. *Apokatastasis* vs. universalism, 60, 257. Origen, 8-9. Decision at the moment of death, 301-302. Matthew 25, 344-345.

Denzinger-Schonmetzer, *Enchiridion Symbolorum, Definitionum et Declarationum* (Freiburg i. B.: Herder, 1963). Hell as a possibility, documents #72, 76, 801, 858 and 1306. Condemnation of Origen, #411. Final decision at moment of death, #858 and 1002.

Meister Eckhart, trans. by Matthew Fox, *Meditations with Meister Eckhart* (Santa Fe: Bear & Co., 1983), 28.

Erik Erikson, *Identity: Youth and Crisis* (New York: W.W. Norton, 1968). Studies of children's play, 268-271. How sexuality affects our perception of God, 293-294.

Charles H. Giblin, "Structural and Theological Considerations on Luke 15," *Catholic Biblical Quarterly*, Vol. 24 (1962), 16.

Carol Gilligan, *In a Different Voice* (Cambridge, MA: Harvard University Press, 1982).

Andrew Greeley, *The Religious Imagination* (New York: William Sadlier, 1981), 23-29 and 209-213.

John Heaney, S.J., *The Sacred and the Psychic* (Ramsey, NJ: Paulist, 1984). Near-death experiences, 129-148.

Gerard Hughes, S.J., *God of Surprises* (London: Darton Longman & Todd Ltd, 1985). Good Old Uncle George, 34.

Walter Imbiorski, quoted in Dick Westley, *Redemptive Intimacy: A New Perspective for the Journey to Adult Faith* (P.O. Box 180, Mystic, CT 06355, 1-800-321-0411: Twenty-Third Publications, 1981), 111-112.

Joachim Jeremias, *The Proclamation of Jesus* (New York: Charles Scribner's Sons, 1972), 116-117.

The New Jerusalem Bible (Garden City: Doubleday, 1985). Jesus' descent into hell, footnote h to 1 Peter 3:19. Fallen angels, footnote a to Genesis 6.

Robert Jewett, *Jesus Against the Rapture* (Philadelphia: Westminster Press, 1979), 51-65.

John Paul I, speaking on September 10, 1978. Complete text may be found under the title "Praying for Peace," in Matthew O'Connell (ed.), *The Pope Speaks* (Huntington, IN: Sunday Visitor), 23:4, 314.

John Paul II, encyclical "Rich in Mercy," note #52.

Elisabeth Kübler-Ross, quoted in Plowboy, "The Plowboy Interview: Elisabeth Kübler-Ross on Living, Dying . . . and Beyond," *The Mother Earth News,* May-June, 1983.

Hans Küng, *Eternal Life?* translated by Edward Quinn (Garden City: Doubleday, 1984). Decision at death, 137. Quote from Thomas & Gertrude Sartory, 132.

George Maloney, *The Everlasting Now* (Notre Dame: Ave Maria, 1980), 111.

Richard McBrien, *Catholicism* (Study Edition) (Minneapolis: Winston, 1981), 1152.

Alice Miller, *Banished Knowledge* (New York: Doubleday, 1990), 33 & 35.

Raymond Moody, *Life After Life* (Covington, GA: Mockingbird, 1975).

Raymond Moody, *Reflections on Life After Life* (New York: Bantam, 1977).

NCR (October 9, 1992), 5.

James Nelson, "Male Sexuality and Masculine Spirituality," in *SIECUS* Report, 13:4 (March, 1985), 1–4.

David Nygren and Miriam Ukeritis, study reported in the *Minneapolis Star Tribune* (October 10, 1992), 10E.

Daniel J. O'Hanlon, S.J., "Integration of Christian Practices: A Western Christian Looks East," *Studies in the Spirituality of Jesuits* (May, 1984), 10–11.

Karl Rahner, "The Hermeneutics of Eschatalogical Assertions," in *Theological Investigations*, Vol. IV (Baltimore: Helicon, 1966). On need for reformulation of dogma.

Karl Rahner, S.J. (ed.), *Sacramentum Mundi: An Encyclopedia of Theology, Vol. I* (New York: Herder & Herder, 1968), "Apocatastasis," on whether anyone goes to hell. "Hell," on metaphors for perdition (see also "Gehinnom," in *The Universal Jewish Encyclopedia*, Vol. 4 (New York: Ktav, 1969), 520–521; J.L. McKenzie, *Dictionary of the Bible* (Milwaukee: Bruce, 1965), 300, 801; Dalton, 17–73).

Rosemary Radford Reuther, "Envisioning Our Hopes: Some Models of the Future," in Kalven & Buckley (eds.), *Women's Spirit Bonding* (New York: Pilgrim Press, 1984), 335.

Kenneth Ring, *Life at Death: A Scientific Investigation of Near-Death Experience* (New York: Coward, McCann & Geoghegan, 1980).

John A. T. Robinson, *In the End God* (New York: Harper & Row, 1968). Further chance after death, 44. Resurrection of the body, 100. Road that leads to hell, 133.

Carl Rogers, *On Becoming a Person* (Boston: Houghton Mifflin, 1961), 104-105.

Richard Rohr, "Biblical Roots of Mercy," talk delivered at the Association of Christian Therapists Conference, September, 1988.

John Sachs, "Universal Salvation and the Problem of Hell," *Theological Studies,* 52 (1991), 227-254. Overview of current Roman Catholic thinking about universal salvation. Consensus of contemporary Catholic theologians, 242. Rahner and free will, 247. Quote from Hans-Jürgen Verweyen, 254.

Peggy Reeves Sanday, "The Socio-Cultural Context of Rape: A Cross-Cultural Study," *The Journal of Social Issues,* 37:4 (1981).

Thomas & Gertrude Sartory, *In der Hölle brennt kein Feuer* (Munich, 1968), 88-89. Translated and quoted in Küng.

Sandra Schneiders, *Women and the Word* (Mahwah, NJ: Paulist Press, 1986). The Trinity, 2-3. Jesus taking over his Father's trade, 42-44.

Piet Schoonenberg, S.J., "I Believe in Eternal Life," *Concilium, Dogma, the Problem of Eschatology* (New York: Herder & Herder, 1969), 110.

Paul Smith, "Lecture Notes on the Christian Doctrine of Ultimate Reconciliation," Kansas City, MO (January, 1989), 32.

Dr. Robert Stuckey, M.D., "You Gotta Have Hope," *New Catholic World,* Vol. 232, No 1390 (July/August, 1989). Interventions, 160-161. Image of God, 161-162.

Paul Tillich, "The Last Dimension," in George Brantl (ed.), *The Religious Experience* (New York: Braziller, 1964), 590.

Paul Tournier, *Guilt & Grace* (San Francisco: Harper & Row, 1983), 189-197.

Hans Urs von Balthasar, translated excerpt from "Abstieg zur Hölle," quoted in *The Von Balthasar Reader,* Medard Kehl & Werner Loser (eds.) (New York: Crossroad, 1982). Jesus' descent into hell, 153.

Hans Urs von Balthasar, quoted in John Sachs, "Universal Salvation and the Problem of Hell," *Theological Studies,* 52 (1991). Jesus' descent into hell, 244.

Kallistos Ware, " 'One Body in Christ': Death and the Communion of Saints," *Sobornost,* 3:2 (1981), 184.

Dick Westley, *Redemptive Intimacy* (Mystic, CT: Twenty-Third Publications, 1981). For how Anselmian salvation theology repesents only one of three dominant New Testament theologies, see 112ff.

Elie Wiesel, *Night* (Bantam: New York, 1982), 61ff.

(Re: William Wilson), *As Bill Sees It* (New York: Alcoholics Anonymous World Services, 1967). Only love can heal, 98.

(Re: William Wilson), *'Pass It On'* (New York: Alcoholics Anonymous World Services, 1984). Bill W.'s first drink, 56. Bill's conversion experience, 121.

William Wilson, *Twelve Steps and Twelve Traditions* (New York: Alcoholics Anonymous World Services, 1953). God of belonging, 105.

Pierre Wolf, *May I Hate God?* (Mahwah, NJ: Paulist Press, 1979).

Belonging: Bonds of Healing & Recovery, by Dennis Linn, Sheila Fabricant Linn & Matthew Linn (Mahwah, NJ: Paulist Press, 1993). Twelve Step recovery from any compulsive pattern is integrated with contemporary spirituality and psychology. Defines addiction as our best attempt to belong to ourselves, others, God and the universe, and helps the reader discover the genius underneath every addiction. Chapter 9, on Step 11, contains an adaptation of some of the material in this book on healing our image of God, as it applies to recovery from addictions.

Healing the Eight Stages of Life, by Matthew Linn, Sheila Fabricant & Dennis Linn (Mahwah, NJ: Paulist Press, 1988). Based on Erik Erikson's developmental system, this book helps to heal hurts and develop gifts at each stage of life, from conception through old age. Includes healing ways our image of God has been formed and deformed at each stage.

Healing of Memories, by Dennis & Matthew Linn (Mahwah, NJ: Paulist Press, 1974). A simple guide to inviting Jesus into our painful memories to help us forgive ourselves and others.

Healing Life's Hurts, by Dennis & Matthew Linn (Mahwah, NJ: Paulist Press, 1978). A more thorough book to help the reader move through hurts using the five stages of forgiveness.

Healing the Greatest Hurt, by Matthew & Dennis Linn and Sheila Fabricant (Mahwah, NJ: Paulist Press, 1985). Healing the deepest hurt most people experience, the loss of a loved one, through learning to give and receive love with the deceased through the Communion of Saints. Chapter 5 and Appendix A contain material on afterlife and the problem of hell.

These and other books by the authors are available from Paulist Press, 997 Macarthur Blvd., Mahwah, NJ 07430, (201) 825-7300.

Tapes & Courses (for use alone, with a companion, or with a group)

Good Goats: Healing Our Image of God, by Dennis Linn, Sheila Fabricant Linn & Matthew Linn (Mahwah, NJ: Paulist Press, 1994). Videotape to accompany this book.

Healing Our Image of God, by Dennis Linn, Sheila Fabricant & Matthew Linn (St. Louis: Christian Video Library, 1985). Set of two audio tapes which may be used to accompany this book.

Belonging: Healing & 12 Step Recovery, by Dennis, Sheila & Matthew Linn (Audio Version / Kansas City, MO: Credence Cassettes, 1992). Audio or videotapes and a course guide to accompany book (see above), for use as a program of recovery.

Healing the Eight Stages of Life, by Matthew Linn, Sheila Fabricant & Dennis Linn (Mahwah, NJ: Paulist Press, 1991). Tapes and a course guide which can be used with book (see above) as a course in healing the life cycle. Available on videotape and in two audio versions, condensed and expanded.

Prayer Course for Healing Life's Hurts, by Matthew & Dennis Linn and Sheila Fabricant (Mahwah, NJ: Paulist Press, 1983). Ways to pray for personal healing that integrate physical, emotional, spiritual and social dimensions. Book includes course guide, and tapes are available in video and audio versions.

Praying with Another for Healing, by Dennis & Matthew Linn and Sheila Fabricant (Mahwah, NJ: Paulist Press, 1984). Guide to praying with another to heal hurts such as sexual abuse, depression, loss of a loved one, etc. Book includes course guide, and tapes are available in video and audio versions. *Healing the Greatest Hurt* (see above) may be used as supplementary reading for the last five of these sessions, which focus on healing of grief.

Dying to Live: Healing through Jesus' Seven Last Words, by Bill & Jean Carr and Dennis & Matthew Linn (Mahwah, NJ: Paulist Press, 1983). How the seven last words of Jesus empower us to fully live the rest of our life. Tapes (available in video or audio versions) may be used with the book *Healing the Dying,* by Mary Jane, Dennis & Matthew Linn (Mahwah, NJ: Paulist Press, 1979).

Audio tapes for all of these courses (except *Belonging* and *Healing Our Image of God*) are available from Paulist Press, 997 Macarthur Blvd., Mahwah, NJ 07430, (201) 825-7300. *Belonging* audio tapes are available from Credence Cassettes, 115 E. Armour Blvd., Kansas City, MO 64111, (800) 444-8910. *Healing Our Image of God* audio tapes are available from Christian Video Library, 3914-A Michigan Ave., St. Louis, MO 63118, (314) 865-0729.

Videotapes for all of these courses (except *Belonging*) may be purchased from Paulist Press. *Belonging* videotapes are available from Credence Cassettes at the above address.

Videotapes on a Donation Basis

To borrow any of the above videotapes, contact Christian Video Library at the above address.

Spanish Books & Tapes

Several of the above books and tapes are available in Spanish. For information, contact Christian Video Library.

Retreats & Conferences

For retreats and conferences by the authors on the material in this book and other topics, contact Dennis, Sheila & Matthew Linn, c/o Re-Member Ministries, 3914-A Michigan Ave., St. Louis, MO 63118, (314) 865-0729.

About the Authors

Dennis, Sheila and Matt Linn work together as a team, integrating physical, emotional and spiritual wholeness, having worked as hospital chaplains and therapists, and currently in leading retreats and spiritual direction. They have taught courses on healing in over thirty countries and in many universities, including a course to doctors accredited by the American Medical Association. Matt and Dennis are the authors of twelve books, the last seven co-authored with Sheila. Their books include *Healing of Memories, Healing Life's Hurts, Healing the Dying* (with Sr. Mary Jane Linn) and *To Heal As Jesus Healed* (with Barbara Shlemon), *Prayer Course for Healing Life's Hurts, Praying with Another for Healing, Healing the Greatest Hurt, Healing the Eight Stages of Life, Belonging: Bonds of Healing & Recovery, Good Goats: Healing Our Image of God* and *Healing Spiritual Abuse and Religious Addiction.* These books have sold over a million copies in English and have been translated into fifteen different languages.

About the Illustrator

Francisco Miranda lives in Mexico City. He has written and illustrated several children's books.